POPE BENEDICT XVI

THE SAINTS

Spiritual Thoughts Series

Introduction by Cardinal José Saraiva Martins

United States Conference of Catholic Bishops
Washington, D.C.

Cover photo: *L'Osservatore Romano*

First printing, October 2008

ISBN: 978-1-60137-055-6

CONTENTS

nowledge of the heart is the wisdom of the saints.

Pope Benedict XVI

INTRODUCTION

n this book are presented the figures of some saints reflected on by Pope Benedict XVI during speeches, homilies, and audiences, or cited and used as examples in his writings that are connected to the letters and encyclicals of his pontificate. We may look upon this volume as an ideal gallery of portraits. Each saint has his or her own characteristics, uniqueness, and traits, distinguishing each one from others and revealing the nearness to God while reflecting the light from one particular perspective. Each of them, in fact, from their personal stories and the circumstances of their earthly lives, demonstrates that "the saint is the person who is so fascinated by the beauty of God and by his perfect truth as to be progressively transformed" (Homily, October 23, 2005). What renders them extraordinarily beautiful is the beauty which the faith places on their countenances and which drives "so many men and women to follow in their footsteps" (Message, May 31, 2006).

Reading these profiles, we realize that the mission of the saints in history can become concrete and efficacious because they "are men and women of faith, hope and love" (*God Is Love* [*Deus Caritas Est*], no. 40). In the action of every day, with its accompanying troubles and difficulties, the saints show themselves to be men of God, who look upon reality with the eyes of faith. That is the case with St. Padre Pio of Pietrelcina, whose "works offer an extraordinary example of the truth that nothing is impossible with God" (Speech, October 14, 2006); likewise with St. Thérèse of Lisieux, "who pointed out trusting abandonment to God's love as the 'simple' way" (Angelus, October 1, 2006). Many times this fidelity coincides exactly with adherence to the will of the Lord. In this context, Pope Benedict sketches out in an extraordinary manner the figures of St. Joseph and Our Lady. He notes, regarding Joseph, his capacity for silence, "a silence woven of constant prayer, a prayer of blessing of the Lord, of the adoration of his holy will and of unreserved entrustment to his providence" (Angelus, December 18, 2005). With regard to Mary, he underscores her sublime intuition of "contribut[ing] to the salvation of the world," not by "carrying out her own projects" but by "plac[ing] herself completely at the disposal of God's initiatives" (*God Is Love* [*Deus Caritas Est*], no. 41).

At other times, the light that the saints spread abroad is that of hope. Such is the case of St. Bakhita, originally a slave in Sudan and then taken to Italy, where she hoped to find less cruel masters; there, she was able to experience in an absolute way that she was loved by God. Thus, rather than returning to her own country, she took up the humble duties of religious life and sought to fulfill her mission: "The hope born in her," comments the Holy Father, "she could not keep to herself; this hope had to reach out to many, to reach everybody" (*On Christian Hope* [*Spe Salvi*], no. 3). At yet other times, the seeds that are sown are those of charity. Pope Benedict has a particular place in his heart for those who have exercised this virtue in a special way (cf. *God Is Love* [*Deus Caritas Est*], no. 40). A saint who exemplifies this dimension is Martin of Tours, who made his own the logic of sharing "to authentically explain love of neighbor" (Angelus, November 11, 2007). In fact, at the city gates of Amiens, he cut his mantle in half for a pauper; that night, Jesus appeared to him in a dream, dressed in that very same mantle. And so, he began to think that it is this very gesture of love which makes the sun warm not only in St. Martin's summer[1] but in any season of man.

If one considers what Pope Benedict proposes in the light of the stories of the saints, we realize that he continually recalls to men and women the model of a sanctity that is possible. The saints are not only an outstanding band of the elect or only those officially recognized by the Church, but all those baptized of every time and place of the earth who, with fidelity and love, have sought to do God's will: "being a Saint"—explains the Pope in formidable fashion—"means living close to God, to live in his family" (Homily, November 1, 2006). To become holy (cf. 1 Pt 1:14) means establishing ever more a proximity to God, rediscovering ever more his light within us, and allowing him to come to enlighten our conscience and to illumine ever more abundantly the spaces within our ego. And all this is possible and always will be possible, the Holy Father teaches us constantly in his instructions, if we look to the Son, if we learn to listen to him and to believe in him, following him docilely and doing his will, the will of God.

---

[1] ["St. Martin's summer" is similar to "Indian summer." Since his feast occurs on November 11, it is presumed that summer would be over by then.—Ed.]

It is in this way, in fact, that every person can move toward holiness: "the secret of holiness," says the Pope, addressing the young people in Cologne for World Youth Day in 2005, "is friendship with Christ and faithful obedience to his will" (Speech, August 19, 2005).

Jesus tells us so many things about holiness; indeed, he tells us everything about holiness. But in his encounters with sinners along the byways of Galilee—which are in reality the byways of the world and of life, to us limited creatures, constantly threatened by sin and constantly exposed to the limits of our human condition—Jesus recalls above all, like a loving father, that being holy does not mean being perfect. He never tires of whispering to our hearts that holiness does not consist in not ever having erred or sinned. If we conform ourselves to the teaching of Jesus, we discover rather that holiness consists in having the desire to forgive, to begin again, to make a gift of ourselves, to forego or take up, with the result that we render ever more concrete the life of Christ by our conduct. Thus, in an extraordinary manner, Pope Benedict illustrates this dynamic principle of spirituality: "holiness increases with the capacity for conversion, repentance, willingness to begin again, and above all with the capacity for reconciliation and forgiveness. . . . Thus, what makes us holy is not never having erred, but the capacity for reconciliation and pardon. And all of us can learn this road to holiness" (General Audience, January 31, 2007).

Pope John Paul II said that holiness is the principal way forward for believers of the third millennium (cf. General

Audience, May 16, 2001). The stories of the saints collected in this volume tell of men and women who, obedient to the divine plan, sometimes had to confront trials and indescribable sufferings, persecutions and martyrdom. Pope Benedict XVI reminds us that "every form of holiness, even if it follows different paths, always passes through the Way of the Cross, the way of self-denial" (Homily, November 1, 2006) and thus offers us likewise the key that opens up for us the interpretation of our whole life. Holiness does not ignore or diminish the Cross, renunciation, and self-donation. Only in this state can holiness truly become our common aspiration and realize in man the true ideal of happiness so often misunderstood and bartered in our age with tired idols that can only sadden man. And so, says Pope Benedict, the blessed ones and the saints point out to us the way to become happy and show us how to be truly human persons because they "did not doggedly seek their own happiness, but simply wanted to give themselves, because the light of Christ had shone upon them" (Speech, August 20, 2005). In reality, the only form of happiness possible is holiness; this is the definitive message which Pope Benedict invites us to take into our lives and to perceive on the countenances of the saints who, with their ongoing work, contribute to the formation of the truest and most precious treasure "of the Church and of all who are in search of the Gospel truth and perfection" (Message, April 27, 2006).

Cardinal José Saraiva Martins
Prefect, Congregation for the Causes of Saints

THE SAINTS

St. Albert Hurtado Cruchaga, SJ

(1901–1952; AUGUST 18)

Program of action

"You shall love the Lord your God with your whole heart. . . . You shall love your neighbor as yourself" (Mt 22:37, 39). This was the program of life of St. Albert Hurtado, who wished to identify himself with the Lord and to love the poor with this same love. The formation received in the Society of Jesus, strengthened by prayer and adoration of the Eucharist, allowed him to be won over by Christ, being a true contemplative in action. In love and in the total gift of self to God's will, he found strength for the apostolate. He founded *El Hogar de Cristo* for the most needy and the homeless, offering them a family atmosphere full of human warmth. In his priestly ministry he was distinguished for his simplicity and availability towards others, being a living image of the Teacher, "meek and humble of heart." In his last days, amid the strong pains caused by illness, he still had the strength to repeat, "I am content, Lord," thus expressing the joy with which he always lived.

> *Homily at Mass for the canonization of*
> *St. Albert Hurtado Cruchaga, SJ, and others*
> *October 23, 2005*

St. Ambrose

(C. 340–397: DECEMBER 7)

Ambrosian catechesis

[St. Augustine tells us that] Ambrose read the Scriptures with his mouth shut, only with his eyes (cf. *Confessions*, 6, 3). Indeed, in the early Christian centuries reading was conceived of strictly for proclamation, and reading aloud also facilitated the reader's understanding. That Ambrose could scan the pages with his eyes alone suggested to the admiring Augustine a rare ability for reading and familiarity with the Scriptures. Well, in that "reading under one's breath," where the heart is committed to achieving knowledge of the Word of God . . . one can glimpse the method of Ambrosian catechesis; it is Scripture itself, intimately assimilated, which suggests the content to proclaim that will lead to the conversion of hearts. Thus, with regard to the magisterium of Ambrose and of Augustine, catechesis is inseparable from witness of life. What I wrote on the theologian in the *Introduction to Christianity* might also be useful to the catechist. An educator in the faith cannot risk appearing like a sort of clown who recites a part "by profession." Rather—to use an image dear to Origen, a writer who was particularly appreciated by Ambrose—he must be like the beloved disciple who rested his head against his

Master's heart and there learned the way to think, speak and act. The true disciple is ultimately the one whose proclamation of the Gospel is the most credible and effective.

General Audience
October 24, 2007

St. Andrew the Apostle

(FIRST CENTURY; NOVEMBER 30)

The "first-called"

Andrew had previously been a disciple of John the Baptist: and this shows us that he was a man who was searching, who shared in Israel's hope, who wanted to know better the word of the Lord, the presence of the Lord. He was truly a man of faith and hope; and one day he heard John the Baptist proclaiming Jesus as "the Lamb of God" (Jn 1:36); so he was stirred, and with another unnamed disciple followed Jesus, the one whom John had called "the Lamb of God." The Evangelist says that "they saw where he was staying; and they stayed with him that day . . ." (Jn 1:37-39). Thus, Andrew enjoyed precious moments of intimacy with Jesus. The account continues with one important annotation: "One of the two who heard John speak, and followed him, was Andrew, Simon Peter's brother. He first found his brother Simon, and said to him, 'We have found the Messiah' (which means Christ). He brought him to Jesus" (Jn 1:40-43), straightaway showing an unusual apostolic spirit. Andrew, then, was the first of the Apostles to be called to follow Jesus. Exactly for this reason the liturgy of the Byzantine Church honors him with the nickname: "*Protokletos*" [protoclete], which means, precisely, "the first called."

General Audience
June 14, 2006

St. Anselm of Canterbury

(1033–1109; APRIL 21)

Passion for the truth

If the question of the truth and the concrete possibility for every person to be able to reach it is neglected, life ends up being reduced to a plethora of hypotheses, deprived of assurances and points of reference. As the famous humanist Erasmus once said: "Opinions are the source of happiness at a cheap price! To understand the true essence of things, even if it treats of things of minimal importance, costs great endeavor" (cf. *The Praise of Folly*, XL, VII). . . . This endeavor, however, enables one to enter progressively into the heart of questions and to open oneself to passion for the truth and to the joy of finding it. The words of the holy Bishop Anselm of Aosta remain totally current: "That I may seek you desiring you, that I may desire you seeking you, that I may find you loving you, and that loving you I may find you again" (cf. *Proslogion*, 1).

Visit to the Pontifical Lateran University
October 21, 2006

St. Anthony of St. Anne Galvão

(1739–1822; DECEMBER 23)

The example of Brother Galvão

The significance of Frei Galvão's example lies in his willingness to be of service to the people whenever he was asked. He was renowned as a counselor, he was a bringer of peace to souls and families, and a dispenser of charity especially towards the poor and the sick. He was greatly sought out as a confessor, because he was zealous, wise and prudent. It is characteristic of those who truly love that they do not want the Beloved to be offended; the conversion of sinners was therefore the great passion of our saint. Sr. Helena Maria, the first religious sister destined to belong to the *Recolhimento de Nossa Senhora da Conceição*, witnessed to what Frei Galvão had said to her: "*Pray that the Lord our God will raise sinners with his mighty arm from the wretched depths of the sins in which they find themselves.*" May this insightful admonition serve as a stimulus to us to recognize in the Divine Mercy the path towards reconciliation with God and our neighbor, for the peace of our consciences.

> *Homily at Mass for the canonization*
> *of St. Anthony of St. Anne Galvão*
> *May 11, 2007*

Archangels Michael, Gabriel, and Raphael

(SEPTEMBER 29)

The messengers of God

The three Archangels who are mentioned by name in Scripture [are] Michael, Gabriel and Raphael. . . . But what is an Angel? Sacred Scripture and the Church's tradition enable us to discern two aspects. On the one hand, the Angel is a creature who stands before God, oriented to God with his whole being. All three names of the Archangels end with the word "*El,*" which means "God." God is inscribed in their names, in their nature. Their true nature is existing in his sight and for him. In this very way the second aspect that characterizes Angels is also explained: they are God's messengers. They bring God to men, they open heaven and thus open earth. Precisely because they are with God, they can also be very close to man. Indeed, God is closer to each one of us than we ourselves are. The Angels speak to man of what constitutes his true being, of what in his life is so often concealed and buried. They bring him back to himself, touching him on God's behalf. In this sense, we human beings must also always return to being angels to one another—angels who turn people away from erroneous ways and direct them always, ever anew, to God.

Homily at Mass for the ordination of six new bishops
September 29, 2007

St. Athanasius

"God-with-us"

Athanasius was undoubtedly one of the most important and revered early Church Fathers. But this great Saint was above all the impassioned theologian of the Incarnation of the *Logos*, the Word of God who—as the Prologue of the fourth Gospel says—"became flesh and dwelt among us" (Jn 1:14). . . . The most famous doctrinal work of the holy Alexandrian Bishop is his treatise: *De Incarnatione*, *On the Incarnation of the Word*, the divine *Logos* who was made flesh, becoming like one of us for our salvation. In this work Athanasius says with an affirmation that has rightly become famous that the Word of God "was made man so that we might be made God; and he manifested himself through a body so that we might receive the idea of the unseen Father; and he endured the insolence of men that we might inherit immortality" (54, 3). With his Resurrection, in fact, the Lord banished death from us like "straw from the fire" (8, 4). The fundamental idea of Athanasius's entire theological battle was precisely that God is accessible. He is not a secondary God, he is the true God, and it is through our communion with Christ that we can truly be united to God. He has really become "God-with-us."

General Audience
June 20, 2007

St. Augustine

(354–430; AUGUST 28)

The doctor of grace

St. Augustine was a man driven by a tireless desire to find the truth, to find out what life is, to know how to live, to know man. And precisely because of his passion for the human being, he necessarily sought God, because it is only in the light of God that the greatness of the human being and the beauty of the adventure of being human can fully appear. At first, this God appeared very remote to him. Then Augustine found him: this great and inaccessible God made himself close, one of us. The great God is our God, he is a God with a human face. Thus, his faith in Christ did not have its ultimate end in his philosophy or in his intellectual daring, but on the contrary, impelled him further to seek the depths of the human being and to help others to live well, to find life, the art of living. This was his philosophy: to know how to live with all the reason and all the depths of our thought, of our will, and to allow ourselves to be guided on the path of truth, which is a path of courage, humility and permanent purification. Faith in Christ brought all Augustine's seeking to fulfillment, but fulfillment in the sense that he always remained on the way. Indeed, he tells us: even in eternity our seeking will not be completed, it will be an eternal adventure, the discovery of new greatness, new beauty. He interpreted the words of the Psalm "Seek his face continually," and said: this is true for eternity; and the beauty of eternity is that it is not a static reality but immense progress in the immense beauty of God. Thus, he could discover God as the founding reason, but also as love which embraces us, guides us and gives meaning to history and to our personal life.

Meeting with representatives of the
world of culture in Pavia, Italy
April 22, 2007

St. Barnabas

Saints

Barnabas means "son of encouragement" (Acts 4:36) or "son of consolation." He was a Levite Jew, a native of Cyprus, and this was his nickname. Having settled in Jerusalem, he was one of the first to embrace Christianity after the Lord's Resurrection. With immense generosity, he sold a field which belonged to him, and gave the money to the Apostles for the Church's needs (Acts 4:37). It was he who vouched for the sincerity of Saul's conversion before the Jerusalem community that still feared its former persecutor (cf. Acts 9:27). Sent to Antioch in Syria, he went to meet Paul in Tarsus, where he had withdrawn, and spent a whole year with him there, dedicated to the evangelization of that important city in whose Church Barnabas was known as a prophet and teacher (cf. Acts 13:1). At the time of the first conversions of the Gentiles, therefore, Barnabas realized that Saul's hour had come. As Paul had retired to his native town of Tarsus, he went there to look for him. Thus, at that important moment, Barnabas, as it were, restored Paul to the Church; in this sense he gave back to her the Apostle to the Gentiles. The Church of Antioch sent Barnabas on a mission with Paul, which became known as the Apostle's first missionary journey. . . . The two, Paul and Barnabas, disagreed at the beginning of the second missionary journey because Barnabas was determined to take with them as a companion John called Mark, whereas Paul was against it, since the young man had deserted them during their previous journey (cf. Acts 13:13; 15:36-40). Hence there are also disputes, disagreements and controversies among saints. And I find this very comforting, because we see that the saints have not "fallen from Heaven." They are people like us, who also have complicated problems. Holiness does not consist in never having erred or sinned. Holiness increases the capacity for conversion, for repentance, for willingness to start again and, especially, for reconciliation and forgiveness. So it was that Paul, who had been somewhat harsh and bitter with regard to Mark, in the end found himself with him once again. In St. Paul's last Letters, to Philemon and in his Second Letter to Timothy, Mark actually appears as one of his "fellow workers." Consequently, it is not the fact that we have never erred but our capacity for reconciliation and forgiveness which makes us saints. And we can all learn this way of holiness.

General Audience
January 31, 2007

St. Bartholomew

The extraordinary within the ordinary

We have no precise information about Bartholomew-Nathanael's . . . apostolic activity. According to information handed down by Eusebius, the fourth-century historian, a certain Pantaenus is supposed to have discovered traces of Bartholomew's presence even in India (cf. *Historia ecclesiastica* V, 10, 3). In later tradition, as from the Middle Ages, the account of his death by flaying became very popular. Only think of the famous scene of the *Last Judgment* in the Sistine Chapel in which Michelangelo painted St. Bartholomew, who is holding his own skin in his left hand, on which the artist left his self-portrait. St. Bartholomew's relics are venerated here in Rome in the Church dedicated to him on the Tiber Island, where they are said to have been brought by the German Emperor Otto III in the year 983. To conclude, we can say that despite the scarcity of information about him, St. Bartholomew stands before us to tell us that attachment to Jesus can also be lived and witnessed to without performing sensational deeds. Jesus himself, to whom each one of us is called to dedicate his or her own life and death, is and remains extraordinary.

General Audience
October 4, 2006

SS. Basil and Gregory Nazianzen

(330–379 AND 330–389/390, RESPECTIVELY; JANUARY 2)

Basil: The program of action

Basil spent himself without reserve in faithful service to the Church and in the multiform exercise of the episcopal ministry. In accordance with the program that he himself drafted, he became an "apostle and minister of Christ, steward of God's mysteries, herald of the Kingdom, a model and rule of piety, an eye of the Body of the Church, a Pastor of Christ's sheep, a loving doctor, father and nurse, a cooperator of God, a farmer of God, a builder of God's temple" (cf. *Moralia* 80, 11-20: *PG* 31, 864b-868b).

This is the program which the holy Bishop consigns to preachers of the Word—in the past as in the present—a program which he himself was generously committed to putting into practice. In AD 379 Basil, who was not yet fifty, returned to God "in the hope of eternal life, through Jesus Christ Our Lord" (*De Baptismo*, 1, 2, 9). He was a man who truly lived with his gaze fixed on Christ. He was a man of love for his neighbor. Full of the hope and joy of faith, Basil shows us how to be true Christians.

General Audience
July 4, 2007

Gregory: "The Theologian"

Gregory acquired the nickname: "The Theologian." This is what he is called in the Orthodox Church: the "Theologian." And this is because to his way of thinking theology was not merely human reflection or even less, only a fruit of complicated speculation, but rather sprang from a life of prayer and holiness, from a persevering dialogue with God. And in this very way he causes the reality of God, the mystery of the Trinity, to appear to our reason. In the silence of contemplation, interspersed with wonder at the marvels of the mystery revealed, his soul was engrossed in beauty and divine glory. . . . [Gregory] is a man who makes us aware of God's primacy, hence, also speaks to us, to this world of ours: without God, man loses his grandeur; without God, there is no true humanism. Consequently, let us too listen to this voice and seek to know God's Face.

General Audience
August 8, 2007

St. Benedict, Abbot

(C. 480–543/560: JULY 11)

Quaerere Deum *(To seek God)*

St. Benedict, Patron of Europe, [is] a saint and abbot particularly dear to me as you can guess from my choice of his name. Born in Norcia around 480, Benedict completed his first studies in Rome but, disappointed with city life, withdrew to Subiaco, where for about three years he lived in a grotto—the famous "Sacro Speco"—and dedicated himself entirely to God. Making use of the ruins of a cyclopean villa of the Emperor Nero at Subiaco, he built several monasteries together with his first followers. Thus, he brought into being a fraternal community founded on the primacy of love for Christ, in which prayer and work were alternated harmoniously in praise of God. Some years later, he perfected the form of this project at Monte Cassino and wrote it down in the "Rule," his only work that has come down to us. Seeking among the ashes of the Roman Empire first of all the Kingdom of God, Benedict perhaps unknowingly scattered the seed of a new civilization that would develop, integrating Christian values with the classical heritage on the one hand, and on the other, the Germanic and Slav cultures. . . . I would like to emphasize one typical aspect of his spirituality. Benedict, unlike other great monastic missionaries of his time, did not found a monastic institution whose principal aim was the evangelization of the barbarian peoples; he pointed out to his followers the search for God as the fundamental and indeed, one and only aim of life: "*Quaerere Deum*" [to seek God]. He knew, however, that when the believer enters into a profound relationship with God, he cannot be content with a mediocre life under the banner of a minimalistic ethic and a superficial religiosity. In this light one can understand better the expression that Benedict borrowed from St. Cyprian and summed up in his Rule (IV, 21), the monks' program of life: "*Nihil amori Christi praeponere*," "Prefer nothing to the love of Christ." Holiness consists of this, a sound proposal for every Christian that has become a real and urgent pastoral need in our time, when we feel the need to anchor life and history to sound spiritual references.

Angelus
July 10, 2005

St. Bernadette Soubirous

(1844–1879; APRIL 16)

The Grotto of Lourdes

In presenting herself to Bernadette as the Immaculate Conception, Mary Most Holy came to remind the modern world, which was in danger of forgetting it, of the primacy of divine grace which is stronger than sin and death. And so it was that the site of her apparition, the Grotto of Massabielle at Lourdes, became a focal point that attracts the entire People of God, especially those who feel oppressed and suffering in body and spirit. "Come to me all of you who labor and are heavy laden, and I will give you rest" (Mt 11:28), Jesus said. In Lourdes he continues to repeat this invitation, with the motherly mediation of Mary, to all those who turn to him with trust.

> *Address to the sick at the end of Mass*
> *on the Feast of Our Lady of Lourdes*
> *February 11, 2006*

us in Christ Crucified and Risen. In his love, God heals our will and our sick understanding, raising them to the highest degree of union with him, that is, to holiness and mystical union. St. Bernard deals with this, among other things, in his brief but substantial *Liber de Diligendo Deo*. There is then another writing of his that I would like to point out, *De Consideratione*, addressed to Pope Eugene III. Here, in this very personal book, the dominant theme is the importance of inner recollection . . . an essential element of piety. It is necessary, the Saint observes, to beware of the dangers of excessive activity whatever one's condition and office, because . . . many occupations frequently lead to "hardness of heart," "they are none other than suffering of spirit, loss of understanding, dispersion of grace" (II, 3). This warning applies to every kind of occupation, even those inherent in the government of the Church. In this regard, Bernard addresses provocative words to the Pontiff, a former disciple of his at Clairvaux: "See," he writes, "where these accursed occupations can lead you, if you continue to lose yourself in them . . . without leaving anything of yourself to yourself" (II, 3). How useful this appeal to the primacy of prayer and contemplation is also for us! May we too be helped to put this into practice in our lives by St. Bernard, who knew how to harmonize the monk's aspiration to the solitude and tranquility of the cloister with the pressing needs of important and complex missions at the service of the Church. Let us entrust this desire . . . [that is, the equilibrium between interiority and necessary work] to the intercession of Our Lady, whom he loved from childhood with such a tender and filial devotion as to deserve the title: "Marian Doctor." Let us now invoke her so that she may obtain the gift of true and lasting peace for the whole world. In one of his famous discourses, St. Bernard compares Mary to the Star that navigators seek so as not to lose their course: "Whoever you are who perceive yourself during this mortal existence to be drifting in treacherous waters at the mercy of the winds and the waves rather than walking on firm ground, turn your eyes not away from the splendor of this guiding star, unless you wish to be submerged by the storm! . . . Look at the star, call upon Mary. . . . With her for a guide, you will never go astray; . . . under her protection, you have nothing to fear; if she walks before you, you will not grow weary; if she shows you favor you will reach the goal" (*Hom. Super Missus Est*, II, 17).

Angelus
August 20, 2006

St. Bridget

(1303–1373; JULY 23)

Co-patroness of Europe

St. Bridget [is] one of the women Saints whom John Paul II proclaimed Patroness of Europe. St. Bridget traveled from Sweden to Italy, lived in Rome and also went on pilgrimage to the Holy Land. With her witness she speaks of openness to different peoples and civilizations. Let us ask her to help humanity today to create large spaces for peace. May she obtain from the Lord in particular peace in the Holy Land, for which she felt such deep affection and veneration.

Angelus
July 23, 2006

St. Bruno

(1030–1101; OCTOBER 6)

Silence and contemplation

The mission of St. Bruno, today's saint, is, we might say, interpreted in the prayer for this day, which reminds us, despite being somewhat different in the Italian text, that his mission was silence and contemplation.

But silence and contemplation have a purpose: they serve, in the distractions of daily life, to preserve permanent union with God. This is their purpose: that union with God may always be present in our souls and may transform our entire being.

Silence and contemplation, characteristic of St. Bruno, help us find this profound, continuous union with God in the distractions of every day. Silence and contemplation: speaking is the beautiful vocation of the theologian. This is his mission: in the loquacity of our day and of other times, in the plethora of words, to make the essential words heard. Through words, it means making present the Word, the Word who comes from God, the Word who is God.

> *Homily at Mass with the members of the*
> *International Theological Commission*
> *October 6, 2006*

St. Charles Borromeo

(1538–1584: NOVEMBER 4)

Humility

The Gospel tells us that love, born in God's heart and working through man's heart, is the power that renews the world. This truth shines out in a special way in the testimony of the Saint whose Memorial is celebrated today: Charles Borromeo, Archbishop of Milan. His figure stands out in the sixteenth century as a model of an exemplary Pastor because of his charity, doctrine, apostolic zeal and above all, his prayer. "Souls are won," he said, "on one's knees." Charles Borromeo was consecrated a Bishop when he was only twenty-five years old. He enforced the teaching of the Council of Trent that obliged Pastors to reside in their respective dioceses, and gave himself heart and soul to the Ambrosian Church. He traveled up and down his Diocese three times; he convoked six provincial and eleven diocesan synods; he founded seminaries to train a new generation of priests; he built hospitals and earmarked his family riches for the service of the poor; [he defended the rights of the Church against the powerful;] he renewed religious life and founded a new congregation of secular priests, the Oblates. In 1576, when the plague was raging in Milan, he visited, comforted and spent all his money on the sick. His motto consisted in one word: "*Humilitas*."

It was humility that motivated him, like the Lord Jesus, to renounce himself in order to make himself the servant of all.

Angelus
November 4, 2007

St. Charles of St. Andrew Houben

(1821–1893; JANUARY 5)

The care of souls

"The love of God has been poured into our hearts by the Holy Spirit which has been given us." Truly, in the case of the Passionist priest, *Charles of St. Andrew Houben*, we see how that love overflowed in a life totally dedicated to the care of souls. During his many years of priestly ministry in England and Ireland, the people flocked to him to seek out his wise counsel, his compassionate care and his healing touch. In the sick and the suffering he recognized the face of the Crucified Christ, to whom he had a lifelong devotion. He drank deeply from the rivers of living water that poured forth from the side of the Pierced One, and in the power of the Spirit he bore witness before the world to the Father's love. At the funeral of this much-loved priest, affectionately known as Fr. Charles of Mount Argus, his superior was moved to observe: "The people have already declared him a saint."

> *Homily at Mass for the canonization of*
> *St. Charles of St. Andrew Houben and others*
> *June 3, 2007*

St. Chromatius of Aquileia

(C. 345–407; DECEMBER 2)

Listening to the Word

Chromatius was born in Aquileia in about AD 345. He was ordained a deacon, then a priest; finally, he was appointed Bishop of that Church (388). After receiving episcopal ordination from Bishop Ambrose he dedicated himself courageously and energetically to an immense task because of the vast territory entrusted to his pastoral care: the ecclesiastical jurisdiction of Aquileia, in fact, stretched from the present-day territories of Switzerland, Bavaria, Austria and Slovenia, as far as Hungary. How well known and highly esteemed Chromatius was in the Church of his time we can deduce from an episode in the life of St. John Chrysostom. When the Bishop of Constantinople [Chrysostom] was exiled from his See, he wrote three letters to those he considered the most important Bishops of the West seeking to obtain their support with the Emperors: he wrote one letter to the Bishop of Rome, the second to the Bishop of Milan and the third to the Bishop of Aquileia, precisely, Chromatius (*Ep*. CLV: *PG* LII, 702). Those were difficult times also for Chromatius because of the precarious political situation. In all likelihood Chromatius died in exile, in Grado, while he was attempting to escape the incursions of the Barbarians in 407, the same year when Chrysostom also died. . . . Chromatius was a wise *teacher* and a zealous *pastor*. His first and main commitment was to listen to the Word, to be able to subsequently proclaim it: he always bases his teaching on the Word of God and constantly returns to it.

General Audience
December 5, 2007

St. Clare

(1193/1194–1253: AUGUST 11)

Living the Gospel

On the pathways of the world, Jesus is "the hand" that the Father stretches out to sinners; he is the way that leads to peace (cf. *Second Eucharistic Prayer for Reconciliation*). Truly we discover here that the beauty of creation and the love of God are inseparable. Francis and Clare of Assisi also discover this secret and they propose to their beloved sons and daughters one very simple thing: to live the Gospel. This is their norm of conduct and their rule of life. Clare expressed it very well when she said to her sisters: "Among yourselves, my daughters, let there be the same love with which Christ has loved you" (*Testament*).

Meeting with Poor Clares in Brazil
May 12, 2007

St. Clement

(D. 101; NOVEMBER 23)

The imperative of moral commitment

St. Clement, Bishop of Rome in the last years of the first century, was the third Successor of Peter, after Linus and Anacletus. The most important testimony concerning his life comes from St. Irenaeus, Bishop of Lyons until 202. He attests that Clement "had seen the blessed Apostles," "had been conversant with them," and "might be said to have the preaching of the apostles still echoing [in his ears], and their traditions before his eyes" (*Adversus Haer.* 3, 3, 3). Later testimonies which date back to between the fourth and sixth centuries attribute to Clement the title of martyr. The authority and prestige of this Bishop of Rome were such that various writings were attributed to him, but the only one that is certainly his is the *Letter to the Corinthians*. . . . Clement's Letter touches on topics that were dear to St. Paul, who had written two important Letters to the Corinthians, in particular the theological dialectic, perennially current, between the *indicative* of salvation and the *imperative* of moral commitment. First of all came the joyful proclamation of saving grace. The Lord forewarns us and gives us his forgiveness, gives us his love and the grace to be Christians, his brothers and sisters. It is a proclamation that fills our life with joy and gives certainty to our action: the Lord always forewarns us with his goodness and the Lord's goodness is always greater than all our sins. However, we must commit ourselves in a way that is consistent with the gift received and respond to the proclamation of salvation with a generous and courageous journey of conversion.

General Audience
March 7, 2007

St. Cyril of Alexandria

(370–444; JUNE 27)

Trust in Jesus

The Christian faith is first and foremost the encounter with Jesus, "a Person, which gives life a new horizon" (*Deus Caritas Est*, no. 1). St. Cyril of Alexandria was an unflagging, staunch witness of Jesus Christ, the Incarnate Word of God, emphasizing above all his unity, as he repeats in 433 in his first letter (*PG* 77, 228-237) to Bishop Succensus: "Only one is the Son, only one the Lord Jesus Christ, both before the Incarnation and after the Incarnation. Indeed, the *Logos* born of God the Father was not one Son and the one born of the Blessed Virgin another; but we believe that the very One who was born before the ages was also born according to the flesh and of a woman." Over and above its doctrinal meaning, this assertion shows that faith in Jesus the *Logos* born of the Father is firmly rooted in history because, as St. Cyril affirms, this same Jesus came in time with his birth from Mary, the *Theotòkos*, and in accordance with his promise will always be with us. And this is important: God is eternal, he is born of a woman, and he stays with us every day. In this trust we live, in this trust we find the way for our life.

General Audience
October 3, 2007

St. Cyril of Jerusalem

(315–387; MARCH 18)

In the net of Jesus

The basis of [St. Cyril's] instruction on the Christian faith also served to play a polemic role against pagans, Judaeo Christians and Manicheans. The argument was based on the fulfillment of the Old Testament promises, in a language rich in imagery. Catechesis marked an important moment in the broader context of the whole life—particularly liturgical—of the Christian community, in whose maternal womb the gestation of the future faithful took place, accompanied by prayer and the witness of the brethren. Taken as a whole, Cyril's homilies form a systematic catechesis on the Christian's rebirth through Baptism. He tells the catechumen: "You have been caught in the nets of the Church (cf. Mt 13:47). Be taken alive, therefore; do not escape for it is Jesus who is fishing for you, not in order to kill you but to resurrect you after death. Indeed, you must die and rise again (cf. Rom 6:11, 14). . . . Die to your sins and live to righteousness from this very day" (*Procatechesis*, 5).

General Audience
June 27, 2007

SS. Cyril and Methodius

(NINTH CENTURY; FEBRUARY 14)

The duty of Europe

The example of the two brothers, SS. Cyril and Methodius . . . is a model of dialogue between cultures. It was thanks to their apostolic zeal that the Good News of Christ reached the inhabitants of Central and Eastern Europe in their own language, and a new culture, nourished by the Gospel and the Christian Tradition, was born and was able to develop under their guidance through the liturgy, the law and the institutions, until it became the common good of the Slav peoples. These two apostles, overcoming the rivalry and dissent of the epoch, have shown us the paths of dialogue and unity to be built ceaselessly, and they therefore also became the Patron Saints of Europe. . . . In our uncertain and troubled world, Europe can become a witness and messenger of the necessary dialogue between cultures and religions. Indeed, the history of the Old Continent, deeply marked by divisions and fratricidal wars but also by its efforts to overcome them, invites it to carry out this mission as a response to the expectations of so many men and women in many countries of the world who are still aspiring to development, democracy and religious freedom.

Address to the new ambassador
of Bulgaria to the Holy See
May 13, 2006

St. Daniel Comboni

(354–430; AUGUST 28)

Missionary commitment

The Gospel proclamation remains the first service that the Church owes to humanity in order to offer Christ's salvation to the people of our time, in so many ways humiliated and oppressed, and to give a Christian orientation to the cultural, social and ethical changes that are taking place in the world. This year, a further motive impels us to renewed missionary commitment: the fiftieth anniversary of the Encyclical *Fidei Donum* of the Servant of God Pius XII, which prompted and encouraged cooperation between the Churches for the mission *ad gentes*. I am also pleased to recall that 150 years ago five priests and a layman from Fr. Mazza's Institute in Verona, Italy, set out for Africa, precisely to the present-day Sudan. One of them was St. Daniel Comboni, future Bishop of Central Africa and Patron of those peoples, whose liturgical memorial is celebrated this October 10. Let us entrust all men and women missionaries to the intercession of this Gospel pioneer and to the numerous Missionary Saints and Blesseds.

Angelus
October 7, 2007

St. Elizabeth of Hungary

(1207–1231; NOVEMBER 17)

A European saint

Elizabeth, a "European" Saint, was born into a social context of recent evangelization. Andrew and Gertrude, parents of this authentic pearl of the new Christian Hungary, were careful to instill in her an awareness of her own dignity as God's adoptive daughter. Elizabeth made her own the program of Jesus Christ, Son of God, who in becoming man "emptied himself, taking the form of a servant" (Phil 2:7). Thanks to the help of her excellent teachers, she trod in the footsteps of St. Francis of Assisi and set Christ, the one Redeemer of humanity, as her personal and ultimate goal and model in life. Called to be the wife of the Landgrave of Thuringia, she never ceased to devote herself to the care of the poor, in whom she recognized the likeness of the divine Master. She was able to combine her gifts as an exemplary wife and mother with the exercise of the Gospel virtues that she had learned at the school of the Saint of Assisi. She proved to be a true daughter of the Church, who bore a concrete, visible and meaningful witness to Christ's love. Innumerable people down the ages followed her example, viewing her as a model who mirrored the Christian virtues, lived radically in marriage, in the family and also in widowhood. Political figures have been inspired by her, drawing from her the incentive to work for reconciliation among nations. . . . A deeper knowledge of the personality and work of Elizabeth of Thuringia will help people to rediscover with ever livelier awareness the Christian roots of Hungary and of Europe itself, impelling their leaders to develop the dialogue between the Church and civil society in harmony and respect in order to build a world which is truly free and shows solidarity. May the International Year of Elizabeth be an especially favorable opportunity to highlight for Hungarians, Germans and all Europeans the Christian heritage they have received from their ancestors, so that they may continue to draw from these roots the necessary nourishment for abundant fruitfulness in the new millennium which recently began.

Letter to the primate of Hungary on the eighth
centenary of the birth of St. Elizabeth of Hungary
May 27, 2007

St. Ephrem

(C. 306–373; JUNE 9)

The harp of the Holy Spirit

St. Ephrem was the most characteristic representative of Christianity in the Syriac language. He was born in 306, received his formation from his bishop, and became a deacon in the Church of Nisibi, living virginity and poverty. Because of the Persian occupation, he left his city in 363 to take refuge in Edessa, in modern-day Turkey. His talent, which made him the most famous poet of the patristic era, allowed him to deepen theological reflection through the use of paradoxes, images, and symbols, often inspired by Scripture. His hymns, written for liturgical chant, are meditations on the mysteries of the life of Christ and have strong catechetical value, fostering in the people the internalization of the faith of the Church. Honored by Christian tradition with the title of "harp of the Holy Spirit," Ephrem is a beautiful illustration of a servant. He remained a deacon his whole life long, living out his liturgical ministry, manifesting the love of Christ, about whom he sang in unparalleled fashion, and dedicating himself to charity for the brethren whom he introduced to the content of Revelation. He died in 373, having contracted the plague from the sick for whom he cared.

Adapted from text of General Audience
November 28, 2007

St. Eusebius of Vercelli

(EARLY FOURTH CENTURY TO 371/372; AUGUST 2)

The autonomy of religion from politics

St. Eusebius of Vercelli [is] the first Bishop of Northern Italy of whom we have reliable information. Born in Sardinia at the beginning of the fourth century, he moved to Rome with his family at a tender age. . . . The high esteem that developed around Eusebius explains his election in AD 345 to the Episcopal See of Vercelli. The new Bishop immediately began an intense process of evangelization in a region that was still largely pagan, especially in rural areas. Inspired by St. Athanasius—who had written the *Life of St. Anthony*, the father of monasticism in the East—he founded a priestly community in Vercelli that resembled a monastic community. This coenobium impressed upon the clergy of Northern Italy a significant hallmark of apostolic holiness and inspired important episcopal figures such as Limenius and Honoratus, successors of Eusebius in Vercelli, Gaudentius in Novara, Exuperantius in Tortona, Eustasius in Aosta, Eulogius in Ivrea and Maximus in Turin, all venerated by the Church as saints. With his sound formation in the Nicene faith, Eusebius did his utmost to defend the full divinity of Jesus Christ . . . against the philo-Arian policies of the Emperor. For the Emperor, the simpler Arian faith appeared politically more useful as the ideology of the Empire. For him it was not truth that counted but rather political opportunism: he wanted to exploit religion as the bond of unity for the Empire. . . . Eusebius was consequently condemned to exile, as were so many other Bishops of the East and West. . . . After [the Emperor's] death in 361, Constantius II was succeeded by the Emperor Julian, known as "the Apostate," who was not interested in making Christianity the religion of the Empire but merely wished to restore paganism. He rescinded the banishment of these Bishops and thereby also enabled Eusebius to be reinstated in his See. . . . Eusebius was able to exercise his episcopal ministry for another ten years, until he died, creating an exemplary relationship with his city which did not fail to inspire the pastoral service of other Bishops of Northern Italy . . . such as St. Ambrose of Milan and St. Maximus of Turin. . . . The authentic scale of values—Eusebius's whole life seems to say—does not come from emperors of the past or of today but from Jesus Christ, the perfect Man, equal to the Father in divinity, yet a man like us.

General Audience
October 17, 2007

St. Felix of Nicosia

(1715–1787; MAY 31)

Little things

St. Felix of Nicosia loved to repeat in all situations, joyful or sad: "So be it, for the love of God." In this way we can well understand how intense and concrete his experience was of the love of God, revealed to humankind in Christ. This humble Capuchin Friar, illustrious son of the land of Sicily, austere and penitent, faithful to the most genuine expressions of the Franciscan tradition, was gradually shaped and transformed by God's love, lived and carried out in love of neighbor. Br. Felix helps us to discover the value of the little things that make our lives more precious, and teaches us to understand the meaning of family and of service to our brothers and sisters, showing us that true and lasting joy, for which every human heart yearns, is the fruit of love.

Homily at Mass for the canonization
of St. Felix of Nicosia and others
October 23, 2005

St. Filippo Smaldone

(1848–1923; JUNE 4)

At the service of charity

St. *Filippo Smaldone*, son of South Italy, knew how to instill in his life the higher virtues characteristic of his land. A priest with a great heart nourished continuously on prayer and Eucharistic adoration, he was above all a witness and servant of charity, which he manifested in an eminent way through service to the poor, in particular to deaf-mutes, to whom he dedicated himself entirely. The work that he began developed thanks to the Congregation of the Salesian Sisters of the Sacred Hearts founded by him and which spread to various parts of Italy and the world. St. Filippo Smaldone saw the image of God reflected in deaf-mutes, and he used to repeat that, just as we prostrate before the Blessed Sacrament, so we should kneel before a deaf-mute. From his example we welcome the invitation to consider the ever indivisible love for the Eucharist and love for one's neighbor. But the true capacity to love the brethren can come only from meeting with the Lord in the Sacrament of the Eucharist.

Homily at Mass for the canonization
of St. Filippo Smaldone and others
October 15, 2006

St. Francis of Assisi

(1182–1226: OCTOBER 4)

"Go, repair my house"

The mission arises from the heart: when one stops to pray before a Crucifix with his glance fixed on that pierced side, he cannot but experience within himself the joy of knowing that he is loved and [having] the desire to love and to make himself an instrument of mercy and reconciliation. This is what happened about eight hundred years ago to the young Francis of Assisi in the little church of San Damiano, which was then dilapidated. From the height of the Cross, now preserved in the Basilica of St. Clare, Francis heard Jesus tell him: "Go, repair my house which, as you see, is all in ruins." That "house" was first of all his own life, which needed repair through authentic conversion; it was the Church, not the one made of stones but living persons, always needing purification; it was all of humanity, in whom God loves to dwell. The mission always initiates from a heart transformed by the love of God, as [witnessed by] the countless stories of saints and martyrs . . . who in different ways have spent their life at the service of the Gospel.

Angelus
October 22, 2006

St. Francis of Paola

(1416–1507; APRIL 2)

The virtues of Francis

We desire to extol the outstanding virtues of the rich spirituality of him who was "a burning and shining lamp" (Jn 5:35). His parents, already advanced in years, had recourse to the intercession of St. Francis of Assisi and rejoiced to see him born, and he imitated that saint's spirit of humility and evangelical poverty, as well as his remarkable love for God and neighbor, and for all creatures; he so excelled in the life of penance that he established by perpetual vow for himself and his confreres the following of the program of Lent throughout the entire year. Everywhere he encouraged the reconciliation of kings and men with the Church and God. Assiduously applying himself to prayer, he constantly meditated on the Passion of the Crucified Jesus, and especially fostered devotion toward the Eucharist and the Virgin Mary. He was truly loved by the people and was frequently called upon as their helper. He opposed kings and other powerful men, warning them without any hesitation of the gravity of their crimes and injustices. He was outstanding in his obedience and filial love for the Sovereign Pontiff and gave him valuable assistance in matters of great difficulty. All this moves us, as it has our various predecessors, to seek the heavenly aid of St. Francis of Paola, for ourselves and for the whole Church, at the same time proposing him to the men of our time as an exemplar of the spiritual life.

Letter to the president of the
Pontifical Council for Justice and Peace
April 2, 2007

St. Francis de Sales

(1567–1622; JANUARY 24)

Rule

St. Francis de Sales . . . pointed out the way of holiness as a call addressed to every state of life, underscoring that not only in a monastery, in a cloister, or in religious life can one arrive on the road to holiness, but in every state in life. Accept this invitation . . . and respond generously in your own situations of life to Christ who calls you to make the Gospel your rule of life.

General Audience
January 24, 2007

St. Francis Xavier

(1506–1552; DECEMBER 3)

Patron of the missions

In speaking of St. Ignatius, I cannot overlook . . . St. Francis
Xavier. . . . Not only is their history interwoven through
long years in Paris and Rome, but a single aspiration—one
might say, a single passion—stirred and sustained them,
even in their different human situations: the passion for
working for the ever greater glory of God-the-Trinity
and for the proclamation of the Gospel of Christ to the
peoples who did not know him. St. Francis Xavier, whom
my Predecessor Pius XI, of venerable memory, proclaimed
the "Patron of Catholic Missions," saw as his own mission "opening new ways of access" to the Gospel "in the
immense Continent of Asia." His apostolate in the Orient
lasted barely ten years, but in the four and a half centuries
that the Society of Jesus has existed it has proven wonderfully fruitful, for his example inspired a multitude of missionary vocations among young Jesuits and he remains a
reference point for the continuation of missionary activity
in the great countries of the Asian Continent.

Address to the Jesuits
April 22, 2006

St. Gaetano Catanoso

(1879–1963: APRIL 4)

Apostle of the Holy Face

St. Gaetano Catanoso was a lover and apostle of the Holy Face of Jesus. "The Holy Face," he affirmed, "is my life. He is my strength." With joyful intuition he joined this devotion to Eucharistic piety. He would say: "If we wish to adore the real Face of Jesus . . . we can find it in the divine Eucharist, where with the Body and Blood of Jesus Christ, the Face of Our Lord is hidden under the white veil of the Host." Daily Mass and frequent adoration of the Sacrament of the Altar were the soul of his priesthood: with ardent and untiring pastoral charity he dedicated himself to preaching, catechesis, the ministry of confession, and to the poor, the sick and the care of priestly vocations. To the Congregation of the Daughters of St. Veronica, Missionaries of the Holy Face, which he founded, he transmitted the spirit of charity, humility and sacrifice which enlivened his entire life.

> *Homily at Mass for the canonization*
> *of St. Gaetano Catanoso and others*
> *October 23, 2005*

St. George Preca

(1880–1962; JULY 26)

The vocation to evangelize

George Preca, born in La Valletta on the Island of Malta, was a friend of Jesus and a witness to the holiness that derives from him. He was a priest totally dedicated to evangelization: by his preaching, his writings, his spiritual direction and the administration of the sacraments and, first and foremost, by the example of his life. The Johannine expression "*Verbum caro factum est*" always directed his soul and his work and thus the Lord could make use of him to give life to a praiseworthy institution, the "Society of Christian Doctrine," whose purpose is to guarantee parishes the qualified service of properly trained and generous catechists. As a profoundly priestly and mystical soul, he poured himself out in effusions of love for God, Jesus, the Virgin Mary and the saints. He liked to repeat: "Lord God, how obliged to you I am! Thank you, Lord God, and forgive me, Lord God!" . . . May St. George Preca help the Church, in Malta and throughout the world, to be always a faithful echo of the voice of Christ, the Incarnate Word.

> *Homily at Mass for the canonization*
> *of St. George Preca and others*
> *June 3, 2007*

St. Gregory the Great

(C. 540–604: SEPTEMBER 3)

Action and contemplation

[The] exceptional, I would say, almost unique figure [of St. Gregory the Great] is an example to hold up both to pastors of the Church and to public administrators: indeed, he was first Prefect and then Bishop of Rome. As an imperial official, he was so distinguished for his administrative talents and moral integrity that he served in the highest civil office, *Praefectus Urbis*, when he was only thirty years old. Within him, however, the vocation to the monastic life was maturing; he embraced it in 574, upon his father's death. The Benedictine Rule then became the backbone of his existence. Even when the Pope sent him as his Representative to the Emperor of the East in Constantinople, he maintained a simple and poor monastic lifestyle. Called back to Rome, Gregory, although living in a monastery, was a close collaborator of Pope Pelagius II, and when the Pope died, the victim of a plague epidemic, Gregory was acclaimed by all as his Successor. He sought in every way to escape this appointment but in the end was obliged to yield. He left the cloister reluctantly and dedicated himself to the community, aware of doing his duty and being a simple and poor "servant of the servants of God." "He is not really humble," he wrote, "who understands that he must be a leader of others by decree of the divine will and yet disdains this pre-eminence. If, on the contrary, he submits to divine dispositions, and does not have the vice of obstinacy, and is prepared to benefit others with those gifts when the highest dignity of governing souls is imposed on him, he must flee from it with his heart, but against his will, he must obey" (*Pastoral Rule*, I, 6). . . . With prophetic foresight, Gregory intuited that a new civilization was being born from the encounter of the Roman legacy with so-called "barbarian" peoples, thanks to the cohesive power and moral elevation of Christianity. Monasticism was proving to be a treasure not only for the Church but for the whole of society. With delicate health but strong moral character St. Gregory the Great carried out intense pastoral and civil action. He left a vast collection of letters, wonderful homilies, a famous commentary on the Book of Job and writings on the life of St. Benedict, as well as numerous liturgical texts, famous for the reform of song that was called "Gregorian," after him. However, his most famous work is certainly the *Pastoral Rule*, which had the same importance for the clergy as the Rule of St. Benedict had for monks in the Middle Ages. The life of a pastor of souls must be a balanced synthesis of contemplation and action, inspired by the love "that rises wonderfully to high things when it is compassionately drawn to the low things of neighbors; and the more kindly it descends to the weak things of this world, the more vigorously it recurs to the things on high" (II, 5). In this ever timely teaching, the Fathers of the Second Vatican Council found inspiration to outline the image of today's Pastor. Let us pray to the Virgin Mary that the example and teaching of St. Gregory the Great may be followed by pastors of the Church and also by those in charge of civil institutions.

Angelus
September 3, 2006

St. Gregory of Nyssa

(C. 335–395; JANUARY 10)

The spiritual life

[St. Gregory of Nyssa] was born in about AD 335. His Christian education was supervised with special care by his brother Basil—whom he called "father and teacher" (*Ep.* 13, 4: *SC* 363, 198)—and by his sister Macrina. He completed his studies, appreciating in particular philosophy and rhetoric. Initially, he devoted himself to teaching and was married. Later, like his brother and sister, he too dedicated himself entirely to the ascetic life. He was subsequently elected Bishop of Nyssa and showed himself to be a zealous Pastor, thereby earning the community's esteem. When he was accused of embezzlement by heretical adversaries, he was obliged for a brief period to abandon his episcopal see but later returned to it triumphant (cf. *Ep.* 6: *SC* 363, 164-170) and continued to be involved in the fight to defend the true faith. . . . Furthermore, Gregory is distinguished for his spiritual doctrine. None of his theology was academic reflection; rather, it was an expression of the spiritual life, of a life of faith lived. As a great "father of mysticism," he pointed out in various treatises . . . the path Christians must take if they are to reach true life, perfection. . . . Man's goal is the contemplation of God. In him alone can he find his fulfillment. To somehow anticipate this goal in this life, he must work ceaselessly toward a spiritual life, a life in dialogue with God. In other words—and this is the most important lesson that St. Gregory of Nyssa has bequeathed to us—total human fulfillment consists in holiness, in a life lived in the encounter with God, which thus becomes luminous also to others and to the world.

General Audience
August 29, 2007

St. Hilary of Poitiers

(315–367; JANUARY 13)

The virtues of fortitude and meekness

St. Hilary of Poitiers [is] one of the important Episcopal figures of the fourth century. In the controversy with the Arians, who considered Jesus the Son of God to be an excellent human creature but only human, Hilary devoted his whole life to defending faith in the divinity of Jesus Christ, Son of God and God as the Father who generated him from eternity. . . . Elected Bishop of his native city around 353-354. . . . in the summer of 356, Hilary was forced to leave Gaul. Banished to Phrygia in present-day Turkey, Hilary found himself in contact with a religious context totally dominated by Arianism. Here too, his concern as a Pastor impelled him to work strenuously to re-establish the unity of the Church on the basis of right faith as formulated by the Council of Nicea. To this end he began to draft his own best-known and most important dogmatic work: *De Trinitate (On the Trinity)*. Hilary explained in it his personal journey towards knowledge of God and took pains to show that not only in the New Testament but also in many Old Testament passages . . . Scripture clearly testifies to the divinity of the Son and his equality with the Father. . . . In 360 or 361, Hilary was finally able to return home from exile and immediately resumed pastoral activity in his Church, but the influence of his magisterium extended in fact far beyond its boundaries. . . . This was precisely his gift: to combine strength in the faith and docility in interpersonal relations. In the last years of his life he also composed the *Treatises on the Psalms*. . . . Hilary met St. Martin on various occasions: the future Bishop of Tours founded a monastery right by Poitiers, which still exists today. Hilary died in 367. His liturgical Memorial is celebrated on January 13. In 1851 Blessed Pius IX proclaimed him a Doctor of the universal Church.

General Audience
October 10, 2007

St. Ignatius of Antioch

(D. C. 107; OCTOBER 17)

The realism of Ignatius

No Church Father has expressed the longing for *union* with Christ and for *life* in him with the intensity of Ignatius. . . . In fact, two spiritual "currents" converge in Ignatius, that of Paul, straining with all his might for *union* with Christ, and that of John, concentrated on *life* in him. In turn, these two currents translate into the *imitation* of Christ, whom Ignatius several times proclaimed as "my" or "our God." Thus, Ignatius implores the Christians of Rome not to prevent his martyrdom since he is impatient "to attain to Jesus Christ." And he explains, "It is better for me to die on behalf of Jesus Christ than to reign over all the ends of the earth. . . . Him I seek, who died for us: him I desire, who rose again for our sake. . . . Permit me to be an imitator of the Passion of my God!" (*Romans*, 5-6). One can perceive in these words on fire with love, the pronounced Christological "realism" typical of the Church of Antioch, more focused than ever on the Incarnation of the Son of God and on his true and concrete humanity: "Jesus Christ," St. Ignatius wrote to the Smyrnaeans, "was *truly* of the seed of David," "he was *truly* born of a virgin," "and was *truly* nailed [to the Cross] for us" (1:1).

General Audience
March 14, 2007

St. Ignatius of Loyola

(1491–1556; JULY 31)

Ad maiorem Dei gloriam *[For the greater glory of God]*

St. Ignatius of Loyola was first and foremost a man of God who in his life put God, his greatest glory and his greatest service, first. He was a profoundly prayerful man for whom the daily celebration of the Eucharist was the heart and crowning point of his day. Thus, he left his followers a precious spiritual legacy that must not be lost or forgotten. Precisely because he was a man of God, St. Ignatius was a faithful servant of the Church, in which he saw and venerated the Bride of the Lord and the Mother of Christians. And the special vow of obedience to the Pope, which he himself describes as "our first and principal foundation" (*MI*, Series III, I, p. 162), was born from his desire to serve the Church in the most beneficial way possible. . . . Naturally, the effort to promote a culture inspired by Gospel values in cordial collaboration with the other ecclesial realities demands an intense spiritual and cultural training. For this very reason, St. Ignatius wanted young Jesuits to be formed for many years in spiritual life and in study. It is good that this tradition be maintained and reinforced, also given the growing complexity and vastness of modern culture. Another of his great concerns was the Christian education and cultural formation of young people: hence, the impetus he gave to the foundation of "colleges," which after his death spread in Europe and throughout the world. Continue, dear Jesuits, this important apostolate, keeping the spirit of your Founder unchanged.

Address to the Jesuits
April 22, 2006

St. Irenaeus of Lyons

(135/140–202/203; JUNE 28)

Against the heretics

The biographical information on [St. Irenaeus of Lyons] comes from his own testimony, handed down to us by Eusebius in his fifth book on Church History. Irenaeus was in all probability born in Smyrna (today, Izmir in Turkey) in about 135-140, where in his youth, he attended the school of Bishop Polycarp, a disciple in his turn of the Apostle John. We do not know when he moved from Asia Minor to Gaul, but his move must have coincided with the first development of the Christian community in Lyons: here, in 177, we find Irenaeus listed in the college of presbyters. In that very year, he was sent to Rome bearing a letter from the community in Lyons to Pope Eleutherius. His mission to Rome saved Irenaeus from the persecution of Marcus Aurelius which took a toll of at least forty-eight martyrs, including the ninety-year-old Bishop Pontinus of Lyons, who died from ill-treatment in prison. Thus, on his return Irenaeus was appointed Bishop of the city. The new Pastor devoted himself without reserve to his episcopal ministry which ended in about 202-203, perhaps with martyrdom. Irenaeus was first and foremost a man of faith and a Pastor. Like a good Pastor, he had a good sense of proportion, of the riches of doctrine and missionary enthusiasm. As a writer, he pursued a twofold aim: to defend true doctrine from the attacks of heretics, and to explain the truth of the faith clearly. His two extant works—the five books of *The*

Detection and Overthrow of the False Gnosis [*Adversus Haereses*] and *Demonstration of the Apostolic Teaching* (which can also be called the oldest "catechism of Christian doctrine")—exactly corresponded with these aims. In short, Irenaeus can be defined as the champion in the fight against heresies.

General Audience
March 28, 2007

St. James

(D. 42: JULY 25)

The traveling Apostle

Early in the first century, in the 40s, King Herod Agrippa, the grandson of Herod the Great, as Luke tells us, "laid violent hands upon some who belonged to the Church. He had James, the brother of John, killed by the sword" (Acts 12:1-2). The brevity of the news, devoid of any narrative detail, reveals on the one hand how normal it was for Christians to witness to the Lord with their own lives, and on the other, that James had a position of relevance in the Church of Jerusalem, partly because of the role he played during Jesus' earthly existence. A later tradition, dating back at least to Isidore of Seville, speaks of a visit he made to Spain to evangelize that important region of the Roman Empire. According to another tradition, it was his body instead that had been taken to Spain, to the city of Santiago de Compostela. As we all know, that place became the object of great veneration and is still the destination of numerous pilgrimages, not only from Europe but from the whole world. This explains the iconographical representation of St. James with the pilgrim's staff and the scroll of the Gospel in hand, typical features of the traveling Apostle dedicated to the proclamation of the "Good News" and characteristics of the pilgrimage of Christian life.

General Audience
June 21, 2006

St. Jerome

(C. 347–419/420; SEPTEMBER 30)

The Word of God

[Jerome] commented on the Word of God; he defended the faith, vigorously opposing various heresies; he urged the monks on to perfection; he taught classical and Christian culture to young students. . . . Jerome's literary studies and vast erudition enabled him to revise and translate many biblical texts: an invaluable undertaking for the Latin Church and for Western culture. On the basis of the original Greek and Hebrew texts [and thanks to the comparison with previous versions,]. . . . taking into account the original Hebrew and Greek texts of the Septuagint, the classical Greek version of the Old Testament that dates back to pre-Christian times, as well as the earlier Latin versions, Jerome was able, with the assistance later of other collaborators, to produce a better translation: this constitutes the so-called "*Vulgate*," the "official" text of the Latin Church. . . .

What can we learn from St. Jerome? It seems to me, this above all: to love the Word of God in Sacred Scripture. St. Jerome said: "Ignorance of the Scriptures is ignorance of Christ." It is therefore important that every Christian live in contact and in personal dialogue with the Word of God given to us in Sacred Scripture. This dialogue with Scripture must always have two dimensions: on the one hand, it must be a truly personal dialogue because God speaks with each one of us through Sacred Scripture and it has a message for each one. We must not read Sacred

Scripture as a word of the past but as the Word of God that is also addressed to us, and we must try to understand what it is that the Lord wants to tell us. However, to avoid falling into individualism, we must bear in mind that the Word of God has been given to us precisely in order to build communion and to join forces in the truth on our journey towards God. Thus, although it is always a personal Word, it is also a Word that builds community, that builds the Church. We must therefore read it in communion with the living Church. The privileged place for reading and listening to the Word of God is the liturgy, in which, celebrating the Word and making Christ's Body present in the Sacrament, we actualize the Word in our lives and make it present among us.

General Audience
November 7, 2007

St. John the Baptist

(FIRST CENTURY: JUNE 24)

The Christian's program of action

St. John the Baptist [is] the only saint whose birth is commemorated because it marked the beginning of the fulfillment of the divine promises: John is that "prophet," identified with Elijah, who was destined to be the immediate precursor of the Messiah, to prepare the people of Israel for his coming (cf. Mt 11:14; 17:10-13). His Feast reminds us that our life is entirely and always "relative" to Christ and is fulfilled by accepting him, the Word, the Light and the Bridegroom, whose voices, lamps and friends we are (cf. Jn 1:1, 23; 1:7-8; 3:29). "He must increase, but I must decrease" (Jn 3:30): the Baptist's words are a program for every Christian.

Angelus
June 25, 2006

St. John Bosco

(1815–1888; JANUARY 31)

Youth and Don Bosco

St. John Bosco [was a] father and teacher of the young to whom he proclaimed the Gospel with tireless zeal. May his example encourage you, dear *young people*, to live your Christian vocation authentically; may it help you, dear *sick people*, to offer up your suffering in union with Christ's for the salvation of humanity; may it sustain you, dear *newlyweds*, in your reciprocal commitment to building your family faithful to the love of God and neighbor.

General Audience
January 31, 2007

St. John Chrysostom

(350?–407: September 13)

From theory to practice

Chrysostom is among the most prolific of the Fathers: 17 treatises, more than 700 authentic homilies, commentaries on Matthew and on Paul (Letters to the Romans, Corinthians, Ephesians and Hebrews) and 241 letters are extant. He was not a speculative theologian. Nevertheless, he passed on the Church's tradition and reliable doctrine in an age of theological controversies, sparked above all by Arianism or, in other words, the denial of Christ's divinity. He is therefore a trustworthy witness of the dogmatic development achieved by the Church from the fourth to the fifth centuries. His is a perfectly pastoral theology in which there is constant concern for consistency between thought expressed via words and existential experience. It is this in particular that forms the main theme of the splendid catecheses with which he prepared catechumens to receive Baptism. On approaching death, he wrote that the value of the human being lies in "exact knowledge of true doctrine and in rectitude of life" (*Letter from Exile*). Both these things, knowledge of truth and rectitude of life, go hand in hand: knowledge has to be expressed in life. All his discourses aimed to develop in the faithful the use of intelligence, of true reason, in order to understand and to put into practice the moral and spiritual requirements of faith.

General Audience
September 19, 2007

St. John of the Cross

(1540/1542–1591; DECEMBER 14)

The Gospel lived from love

At the end of his life, St. John of the Cross loved to repeat that we will be judged on love. What is necessary even today, indeed, especially in this our epoch marked by so many human and spiritual challenges, is for Christians to proclaim with their works the merciful love of God! Every baptized person must "live the Gospel." In fact, many people who do not welcome Christ and his exigent teachings easily are nevertheless sensitive to the witness of those who communicate his message through the concrete witness of charity. Love is a language that directly reaches the heart and opens it to trust. I exhort you, then, as St. Peter did to the first Christians, to be ever ready to reply to anyone who asks you the reason "for the hope that is in you" (1 Pt 3:15).

Address to members of the Italian
voluntary service organizations
February 10, 2007

St. John the Evangelist

(FIRST CENTURY; DECEMBER 27)

Friend of Jesus

According to tradition, John is the "disciple whom Jesus loved," who in the Fourth Gospel laid his head against the Teacher's breast at the Last Supper (cf. Jn 13:23), stood at the foot of the Cross together with the Mother of Jesus (cf. Jn 19:25) and lastly, witnessed both the empty tomb and the presence of the Risen One himself (cf. Jn 20:2; 21:7). We know that this identification is disputed by scholars today, some of whom view him merely as the prototype of a disciple of Jesus. Leaving the exegetes to settle the matter, let us be content here with learning an important lesson for our lives: the Lord wishes to make each one of us a disciple who lives in personal friendship with him. To achieve this, it is not enough to follow him and to listen to him outwardly: it is also necessary to live with him and like him. This is only possible in the context of a relationship of deep familiarity, imbued with the warmth of total trust. This is what happens between friends; for this reason Jesus said one day: "Greater love has no man than this, that a man lay down his life for his friends. . . . No longer do I call you servants, for the servant does not know what his master is doing; but I have called you friends, for all that I have heard from my Father I have made known to you" (Jn 15:13, 15).

General Audience
July 5, 2006

St. Josemaria Escriva de Balaguer

(1902–1975; JUNE 26)

To serve

"Service: how much I like that word!" said St. Josemaria Escriva—and he added, "let us entrust to the Lord our decision to wish to learn how to serve, because only in this way will we be able not only to know Christ but to make him known and loved by others" (*It Is Jesus Who Speaks*, 182).

General Audience
April 4, 2007

St. Joseph

(FIRST CENTURY: MARCH 19)

The silence of St. Joseph

Beloved Pope John Paul II, who was very devoted to St. Joseph, left us a wonderful meditation dedicated to him in the Apostolic Exhortation *Redemptoris Custos*, "The Guardian of the Redeemer." Among the many aspects on which this Document sheds light, the silence of St. Joseph is given a special emphasis. His silence is steeped in contemplation of the mystery of God in an attitude of total availability to the divine desires. In other words, St. Joseph's silence does not express an inner emptiness but, on the contrary, the fullness of the faith he bears in his heart and which guides his every thought and action. It is a silence thanks to which Joseph, in unison with Mary, watches over the Word of God, known through the Sacred Scriptures, continuously comparing it with the events of the life of Jesus; a silence woven of constant prayer, a prayer of blessing of the Lord, of the adoration of his holy will and of unreserved entrustment to his providence. It is no exaggeration to think that it was precisely from his "father" Joseph that Jesus learned—at the human level—that steadfast interiority which is a presupposition of authentic justice, the "superior justice" which he was one day to teach his disciples (cf. Mt 5:20). Let us allow ourselves to be "filled" with St. Joseph's silence! In a world that is often too noisy, that encourages neither recollection nor listening to God's voice, we are in such deep need of it.

Angelus
December 18, 2005

St. Josephine Bakhita

(1868–1947; FEBRUARY 8)

The great hope

I am thinking of the African Josephine Bakhita, canonized by Pope John Paul II. She was born around 1869—she herself did not know the precise date—in Darfur in Sudan. At the age of nine, she was kidnapped by slave-traders, beaten till she bled, and sold five times in the slave-markets of Sudan. Eventually she found herself working as a slave for the mother and the wife of a general, and there she was flogged every day till she bled; as a result of this she bore 144 scars throughout her life. Finally, in 1882, she was bought by an Italian merchant for the Italian consul Callisto Legnani, who returned to Italy as the Mahdists advanced. Here, after the terrifying "masters" who had owned her up to that point, Bakhita came to know a totally different kind of "master"—in Venetian dialect, which she was now learning, she used the name "*paron*" for the living God, the God of Jesus Christ. Up to that time she had known only masters who despised and maltreated her, or at best considered her a useful slave. Now, however, she heard that there is a "*paron*" above all masters, the Lord of all lords, and that this Lord is good, goodness in person. She came to know that this Lord even knew her, that he had created her—that he actually loved her. She too was loved, and by none other than the supreme "*Paron*," before whom all other masters are themselves no more than lowly servants. She was known and loved and she was awaited. What is more, this master had himself accepted the destiny of being flogged and now he was waiting for her "at the Father's right hand." Now she had "hope"—no longer simply the modest hope of finding masters who would be less cruel, but the great hope: "I am definitively loved and whatever happens to me—I am awaited by this Love. And so my life is good." Through the knowledge of this hope she was "redeemed," no longer a slave, but a free child of God. She understood what Paul meant when he reminded the Ephesians that previously they were without hope and without God in the world—without hope *because* without God. Hence, when she was about to be taken back to Sudan, Bakhita refused; she did not wish to be separated again from her "*Paron*." On January 9, 1890, she was baptized and confirmed and received her first Holy Communion from the hands of the Patriarch of Venice. On December 8, 1896, in Verona, she took her vows in the Congregation of the Canossian Sisters and from that time onwards, besides her work in the sacristy and in the porter's lodge at the convent, she made several journeys round Italy in order to promote the missions: the liberation that she had received through her encounter with the God of Jesus Christ, she felt she had to extend, it had to be handed on to others, to the greatest possible number of people. The hope born in her which had "redeemed" her she could not keep to herself; this hope had to reach many, to reach everybody.

Encyclical letter On Christian Hope (Spe Salvi), *no. 3*
November 30, 2007

St. Justin

(100–C. 165; JUNE 1)

The true philosophy

Justin was born in about the year 100 near ancient Shechem, Samaria, in the Holy Land; he spent a long time seeking the truth, moving through the various schools of the Greek philosophical tradition. Finally, as he himself recounts in the first chapters of his *Dialogue with Tryphon*, a mysterious figure, an old man he met on the seashore, initially leads him into a crisis by showing him that it is impossible for the human being to satisfy his aspiration to the divine solely with his own forces. He then pointed out to him the ancient prophets as the people to turn to in order to find the way to God and "true philosophy." In taking his leave, the old man urged him to pray that the gates of light would be opened to him. The story foretells the crucial episode in Justin's life: at the end of a long philosophical journey, a quest for the truth, he arrived at the Christian faith. He founded a school in Rome where, free of charge, he initiated students into the new religion, considered as the true philosophy. Indeed, in it he had found the truth, hence, the art of living virtuously. For this reason he was reported and beheaded in about 165 during the reign of Marcus Aurelius, the philosopher-emperor to whom Justin had actually addressed one of his *Apologia*. . . . In a time like ours, marked by relativism in the discussion on values and on religion—as well as in interreligious dialogue—this is a lesson that should not be forgotten. To this end, I suggest to you once again . . . the last words of the mysterious old man whom Justin the Philosopher met on the seashore: "Pray that, above all things, the gates of light may be opened to you; for these things cannot be perceived or understood by all, but only by the man to whom God and his Christ have imparted wisdom" (*Dialogue with Tryphon*, 7:3).

General Audience
March 21, 2007

St. Marie Eugenie of Jesus Milleret

(1817–1878; MARCH 10)

A model educator

Marie Eugenie Milleret reminds us first of all of the importance of the Eucharist in the Christian life and in spiritual growth. In fact, as she herself emphasizes, her First Holy Communion was an important moment, even if she was unaware of it at the time. Christ, present in the depths of her heart, was working within her, giving her time to follow her own pace and to pursue her inner quest, which was to lead her to the point of giving herself totally to the Lord in the Religious life in response to the needs of her time. In particular, she realized how important it was to pass on to the young generations, especially young girls, an intellectual, moral and spiritual training that would make them adults capable of taking charge of their family life and of making their contribution to the Church and society. Throughout her life she drew the strength for her mission from her life of prayer, ceaselessly combining contemplation and action. May the example of St. Marie Eugenie invite men and women today to pass on to young people values that will help them to become strong adults and joyful witnesses of the Risen One. May young people never be afraid to welcome these moral and spiritual values, living them patiently and faithfully. In this way, they will build their personality and prepare for their future.

Homily at Mass for the canonization of
St. Marie Eugenie of Jesus Milleret and others
June 3, 2007

St. Martin of Tours

(316/317–397; NOVEMBER 11)

The logic of sharing

St. Martin, Bishop of Tours, [is] one of the most celebrated and venerated Saints of Europe. Born of pagan parents in Pannonia, in what is today Hungary, he was directed by his father to a military career around the year 316. Still an adolescent, Martin came into contact with Christianity and, overcoming many difficulties, he enrolled as a catechumen in order to prepare for Baptism. He would receive the Sacrament in his twenties, but he would still stay for a long time in the army, where he would give testimony of his new lifestyle: respectful and inclusive of all, he treated his attendant as a brother and avoided vulgar entertainment. Leaving military service, he went to Poitiers in France near the holy Bishop Hilary. He was ordained a deacon and priest by him, chose the monastic life and with some disciples established the oldest monastery known in Europe at Ligugé. About ten years later, the Christians of Tours, who were without a Pastor, acclaimed him their Bishop. From that time, Martin dedicated himself with ardent zeal to the evangelization of the countryside and the formation of the clergy. While many miracles are attributed to him, St. Martin is known most of all for an act of fraternal charity. While still a young soldier, he met a poor man on the street numb and trembling from the cold. He then took his own cloak and, cutting it in two with his sword, gave half to that man. Jesus appeared to him that night in a dream smiling, dressed in the same cloak.

Dear brothers and sisters, St. Martin's charitable gesture flows from the same logic that drove Jesus to multiply the loaves for the hungry crowd, but most of all to leave himself to humanity as food in the Eucharist, supreme Sign of God's love, *sacramentum caritatis*. It is the logic of sharing which he used to authentically explain love of neighbor. May St. Martin help us to understand that only by means of a common commitment to sharing is it possible to respond to the great challenge of our times: to build a world of peace and justice where each person can live with dignity. This can be achieved if a world model of authentic solidarity prevails which assures to all inhabitants of the planet food, water, necessary medical treatment, and also work and energy resources as well as cultural benefits, scientific and technological knowledge.

Angelus
November 11, 2007

St. Mary

(FIRST CENTURY: SEPTEMBER 12)

The greatness of Mary

Outstanding among the saints is Mary, Mother of the Lord and mirror of all holiness. In the *Gospel of Luke* we find her engaged in a service of charity to her cousin Elizabeth, with whom she remained for "about three months" (1:56) so as to assist her in the final phase of her pregnancy. "*Magnificat anima mea Dominum*," she says on the occasion of that visit, "My soul magnifies the Lord" (Lk 1:46). In these words she expresses her whole program of life: not setting herself at the center, but leaving space for God, who is encountered both in prayer and in service of neighbor—only then does goodness enter the world. Mary's greatness consists in the fact that she wants to magnify God, not herself. She is lowly: her only desire is to be the handmaid of the Lord (cf. Lk 1:38, 48). She knows that she will only contribute to the salvation of the world if, rather than carrying out her own projects, she places herself completely at the disposal of God's initiatives.

Encyclical letter God Is Love (Deus Caritas Est)*, no. 41*
November 30, 2007

St. Mary Magdalene

(FIRST CENTURY; JULY 22)

Disciple of Jesus

St. Mary Magdalene [is] a disciple of the Lord who plays a lead role in the Gospels. St. Luke lists her among the women who followed Jesus after being "healed of evil spirits and infirmities," explaining that "seven demons had gone out" from her (Lk 8:2). Magdalene would be present beneath the Cross with the Mother of Jesus and other women. In the early morning on the first day after the Sabbath she was to be the one to discover the empty tomb, beside which she stood weeping until the Risen Jesus appeared to her (cf. Jn 20:11). The story of Mary of Magdala reminds us all of a fundamental truth: a disciple of Christ is one who, in the experience of human weakness, has had the humility to ask for his help, has been healed by him and has set out following closely after him, becoming a witness of the power of his merciful love that is stronger than sin and death.

Angelus
July 23, 2006

St. Mary Magdalene de' Pazzi

(1566–1607; MAY 25)

The ecstasies of the saint

Born in Florence on April 2, 1566, and baptized at the "beautiful St. John" font with the name Caterina, St. Mary Magdalene de' Pazzi showed a particular sensitivity to the supernatural from childhood and was attracted by intimate colloquy with God. As was the custom for children of noble families, her education was entrusted to the Dames of Malta, in whose monastery she received her First Holy Communion on March 25, 1576, and just some days later she consigned herself to the Lord for ever with a promise of virginity. Returning to her family, she deepened her prayer life with the help of the Jesuit Fathers, who used to come to the palace. She cleverly did not allow herself to be conditioned by the worldly demands of an environment that, although Christian, was not sufficient to satisfy her desire to become more similar to her crucified Spouse. In this context she reached the decision to leave the world and enter the Carmel of St. Mary of the Angels at Borgo San Frediano, where on January 30, 1583, she received the Carmelite habit and the name of Sr. Mary Magdalene. In March of 1584, she fell gravely ill and asked to be able to make her profession prior to the time, and on May 27, Feast of the Trinity, she was carried into the choir on her pallet, where she pronounced before the Lord her vows of chastity, poverty and obedience for ever.

From this moment an intense mystical season began which was also the source of the Saint's great ecstatic fame. The Carmelites of St. Mary of the Angels have five manuscripts in which are recorded the extraordinary experiences of their young Sister. "The Forty Days" of the summer of 1584 are followed by "The Colloquies" of the first half of the following year. The apex of the mystical knowledge that God granted of himself to Sr. Mary Magdalene is found in "Revelations and Intelligences," eight days of splendid ecstasies from the vigil of Pentecost to the Feastday of the Trinity in 1585. This was an intense experience that made her able at only nineteen years of age to span the whole mystery of salvation, from the Incarnation of the Word in the womb of Mary to the descent of the Holy Spirit on Pentecost. Five long years of interior purification followed—Mary Magdalene de' Pazzi speaks of it in the book of "The Probation"—in which her Spouse, the Word, takes away the sentiment of grace and leaves her like Daniel in the lions' den, amid many trials and great temptations. This is the context in which her ardent commitment to renew the Church takes place, after which, in the summer of 1586, splendors of light from on high came to show her the true state of the post-Tridentine era. Like Catherine of Siena, she felt "forced" to write some letters of entreaty to the Pope, Curial Cardinals, her Archbishop and other ecclesial personages, for a decisive commitment to "The Renovation of the Church," as the title of the manuscript that contains them says. It consists of twelve letters dictated in ecstasy, perhaps never sent, but which remain as a testimony of her passion for the *Sponsa Verbi*.

With Pentecost of 1590 her difficult trial ended. She promised to dedicate herself with all her energy to the service of the community and in particular to the formation of novices. Sr. Mary Magdalene had the gift to live communion with God in an ever more interior form, so as to become a reference point for the whole community who still today continue to consider her "mother." The purified love that pulsated in her heart opened her to desire full conformity with Christ, her Spouse, even to sharing with him the "naked suffering" of the Cross. Her last three years of life were a true Calvary of suffering for her. Consumption began to clearly manifest itself: Sr. Mary Magdalene was obliged to withdraw little by little from community life to immerse herself ever more in "naked suffering for love of God." She was oppressed by atrocious physical and spiritual pain which lasted until her death on Friday, May 25, 1607. She passed away at 3 p.m., while an unusual joy pervaded the entire monastery.

Letter to the archbishop of Florence for the fourth centenary of the death of St. Mary Magdalene de' Pazzi
April 29, 2007

St. Matthew

The Evangelist Matthew

The tradition of the ancient Church agrees in attributing to Matthew the paternity of the First Gospel. This had already begun with Bishop Papias of Hierapolis in Frisia, in about the year 130. He writes: "Matthew set down the words (of the Lord) in the Hebrew tongue and everyone interpreted them as best he could" (in Eusebius of Cesarea, *Historia ecclesiastica*, III, 39, 16). Eusebius, the historian, adds this piece of information: "When Matthew, who had first preached among the Jews, decided also to reach out to other peoples, he wrote down the Gospel he preached in his mother tongue; thus, he sought to put in writing, for those whom he was leaving, what they would be losing with his departure" (*Historia ecclesiastica*, III, 24, 6). The Gospel of Matthew written in Hebrew or Aramaic is no longer extant, but in the Greek Gospel that we possess we still continue to hear, in a certain way, the persuasive voice of the publican Matthew, who, having become an Apostle, continues to proclaim God's saving mercy to us. And let us listen to St. Matthew's message, meditating upon it ever anew also to learn to stand up and follow Jesus with determination.

General Audience
August 30, 2006

St. Matthias

(FIRST CENTURY; MAY 14)

Fidelity and witness

We know nothing else about [St. Matthias], if not that he had been a witness to all Jesus' earthly events (cf. Acts 1:21-22), remaining faithful to him to the end. To the greatness of his fidelity was later added the divine call to take the place of Judas, almost compensating for his betrayal. We draw from this a final lesson: while there is no lack of unworthy and traitorous Christians in the Church, it is up to each of us to counterbalance the evil done by them with our clear witness to Jesus Christ, our Lord and Savior.

General Audience
October 18, 2006

St. Maximus of Turin

"The lookout tower" of the city

We come across [St. Maximus] in 398 as Bishop of Turin, a year after St. Ambrose's death. Very little is known about him; in compensation, we have inherited a collection of about ninety of his *Sermons*. It is possible to perceive in them the Bishop's profound and vital bond with his city, which attests to an evident point of contact between the episcopal ministry of Ambrose and that of Maximus. At that time serious tensions were disturbing orderly civil coexistence. In this context, as pastor and teacher, Maximus succeeded in obtaining the Christian people's support. The city was threatened by various groups of barbarians. They entered by the Eastern passes, which went as far as the Western Alps. . . . Maximus' interventions in the face of this situation testify to his commitment to respond to the civil degradation and disintegration. . . . Maximus, with the collapse of the civil authority of the Roman Empire, felt fully authorized in this regard to exercise true control over the city. This control was to become increasingly extensive and effective until it replaced the irresponsible evasion of the magistrates and civil institutions. In this context, Maximus not only strove to rekindle in the faithful the traditional love for their *hometown*, but he also proclaimed the precise duty to pay taxes, however burdensome and unpleasant they might appear (cf. *Sermon* 26, 2). In short, the tone and substance of the *Sermons* imply an increased awareness of the Bishop's political responsibility in the specific historical circumstances. He was "the lookout tower" posted in the city.

General Audience
October 31, 2007

St. Monica

The example of a mother

Monica, who was born into a Christian family at Tagaste, today Souk-Aharàs in Algeria, lived her mission as a wife and mother in an exemplary way, helping her husband Patricius to discover the beauty of faith in Christ and the power of evangelical love, which can overcome evil with good. After his premature death, Monica courageously devoted herself to caring for her three children, including Augustine, who initially caused her suffering with his somewhat rebellious temperament. As Augustine himself was to say, his mother gave birth to him twice; the second time required a lengthy spiritual travail of prayers and tears, but it was crowned at last with the joy of seeing him not only embrace the faith and receive Baptism, but also dedicate himself without reserve to the service of Christ. How many difficulties there are also today in family relations and how many mothers are in anguish at seeing their children setting out on wrong paths! Monica, a woman whose faith was wise and sound, invites them not to lose heart but to persevere in their mission as wives and mothers, keeping firm their trust in God and clinging with perseverance to prayer.

Angelus
August 27, 2006

St. Paulinus of Nola

(C. 335–431; JUNE 22)

The mystery of the unity of the Church

St. Paulinus of Nola was originally from Bordeaux and belonged to one of its wealthiest families. After completing his studies most successfully, he became governor of Campania. Seeing the crowds visiting the tomb of the martyr St. Felix, he converted. He failed miserably in politics but his faith made him say, "Man without Christ is dust and darkness" (*Hymns*, X, 289). He enrolled in the school of St. Ambrose and then completed his theological formation in Bordeaux with the bishop St. Delfinus, from whom he received Baptism. He married a noblewoman of Barcelona, Terasia, with whom he had a son who died a few days after birth. He then felt called to follow Christ totally through a rigorous ascetical life. He withdrew with his wife to Nola, where the couple lived as brother and sister. Paulinus was ordained a priest in Barcelona. Around 409, at the death of the Bishop of Nola, he was chosen as successor. He developed his pastoral plan of action, with particular attention to the poor, leaving an image of an authentic pastor of charity. From his relationship with his instructor Ausonius, he kept his taste for poetry and literature. But it was from Scripture that he took his inspiration and light for daily living. *Lectio divina* led him on the road to perfection. His writings are hymns of faith and love, from which emerges the understanding of the Church as the mystery of unity that carries the faithful to friendship and spiritual communion under the guidance of the Holy Spirit. The witness of Paulinus of Nola helps us understand what the [Second Vatican] Council says when it speaks of the Church as intimate communion with God and of the unity of the human race.

Adapted from text of General Audience
December 12, 2007

St. Peter Damian

(1007–1072; FEBRUARY 21)

Solitude and communion

In his life, St. Peter Damian was proof of a successful synthesis of hermitic and pastoral activity. As a hermit, he
embodied that Gospel radicalism and unreserved love for
Christ, so well expressed in the Rule of St. Benedict: "Prefer
nothing, absolutely nothing, to the love of Christ." As a
man of the Church, he worked with farsighted wisdom and
when necessary also made hard and courageous decisions.
The whole of his human and spiritual life was played out
in the tension between his life as a hermit and his ecclesiastical duty. St. Peter Damian was above all a hermit,
indeed, the last theoretician of the hermitic life in the Latin
Church exactly at the time of the East-West schism. In his
interesting work entitled *The Life of Blessed Romuald*, he
left us one of the most significant fruits of the monastic
experience of the undivided Church. For him, the hermitic
life was a strong call to rally all Christians to the primacy
of Christ and his lordship. It is an invitation to discover
Christ's love for the Church, starting from his relationship
with the Father; a love that the hermit must in turn nour-
ish *with*, *for* and *in* Christ, in regard to the entire People
of God. St. Peter Damian felt the presence of the universal
Church in the hermitic life so strongly that he wrote in
his ecclesiological treatise entitled *Dominus Vobiscum* that
the Church is at the same time one in all and all in each
one of her members. This great holy hermit was also an

eminent man of the Church who made himself available to move from the hermitage to go wherever his presence might be required in order to mediate between contending parties, were they Churchmen, monks or simple faithful. Although he was radically focused on the *unum necessarium*, he did not shirk the practical demands that love for the Church imposed upon him. He was impelled by his desire that the Ecclesial Community always show itself as a holy and immaculate Bride ready for her heavenly Bridegroom, and expressed with a lively *ars oratoria* his sincere and disinterested zeal for the Church's holiness. Yet, after each ecclesial mission he would return to the peace of the hermitage at Fonte Avellana and, free from all ambition, he even reached the point of definitively renouncing the dignity of Cardinal so as not to distance himself from his hermitic solitude, the cell of his hidden existence in Christ. Lastly, St. Peter Damian was the soul of the "*Riforma gregoriana*," which marked the passage from the first to the second millennium and whose heart and driving force was St. Gregory VII. It was, in fact, a matter of the application of institutional decisions of a theological, disciplinary and spiritual character which permitted a greater *libertas Ecclesiae* in the second millennium. They restored the breath of great theology with reference to the Fathers of the Church and in particular, to St. Augustine, St. Jerome and St. Gregory the Great. With his pen and his words he addressed all: he asked his brother hermits for the courage of a radical self-giving to the Lord which would as closely as possible resemble martyrdom; he demanded of the Pope, Bishops and ecclesiastics a high level of evangelical detachment from honors and privileges in carrying out their ecclesial functions; he reminded priests of the highest ideal of their mission that they were to exercise by cultivating purity of morals and true personal poverty. In an age marked by forms of particularism and uncertainties because it was bereft of a unifying principle, Peter Damian, aware of his own limitations—he liked to define himself as *peccator monachus*—passed on to his contemporaries the knowledge that only through a constant harmonious tension between the two fundamental poles of life—solitude and communion—can an effective Christian witness develop. Does not this teaching also apply to our times?

Letter to the Camaldolese Order for
the Feast of St. Peter Damian
February 20, 2007

SS. Peter and Paul

(D. C. 67; JUNE 29)

Catholicity

SS. Peter and Paul, "Apostles of Christ, pillars and foundations of the city of God" . . . [the] liturgy sings. Their martyrdom is considered the true act of birth of the Church of Rome. The two Apostles gave their supreme witness close to each other in time and place: here in Rome, St. Peter was crucified and afterwards St. Paul was decapitated. Their blood mingled as if in a single witness to Christ, which prompted St. Irenaeus, Bishop of Lyons, in the middle of the second century to speak of the "Church founded and organized at Rome by the two most glorious Apostles, Peter and Paul" (*Adversus Haereses* 3, 3, 2). A little later, from North Africa, Tertullian exclaimed: "How happy is the Church of Rome on which the Apostles poured forth all their doctrine along with their blood" (*De Praescriptione Haereticorum*, 36). For this very reason the Bishop of Rome, the Successor of the Apostle Peter, carries out a special ministry at the service of the doctrinal and pastoral unity of the People of God scattered across the world.

Angelus
June 29, 2006

SS. Philip and James

(FIRST CENTURY; MAY 3)

Philip: "Come and see"

The Fourth Gospel recounts that after being called by Jesus, Philip meets Nathanael and tells him: "We have found him of whom Moses in the law and also the prophets wrote, Jesus of Nazareth, the son of Joseph" (Jn 1:45). Philip does not give way to Nathanael's somewhat skeptical answer ("Can anything good come out of Nazareth?") and firmly retorts: "Come and see!" (Jn 1:46). In his dry but clear response, Philip displays the characteristics of a true witness: he is not satisfied with presenting the proclamation theoretically, but directly challenges the person addressing him by suggesting he have a personal experience of what he has been told. . . . According to certain later accounts (*Acts of Philip* and others), our Apostle is said to have evangelized first Greece and then Frisia, where he is supposed to have died, in Hierapolis, by a torture described variously as crucifixion or stoning.

General Audience
September 6, 2006

James: Faith and works

The oldest information on the death of this James is given to us by the Jewish historian Flavius Josephus. In his Jewish Antiquities (20, 201ff.), written in Rome towards the end of the first century, he says that the death of James was decided with an illegal initiative by the High Priest Ananus, a son of the Ananias attested to in the Gospels; in the year 62, [Ananus] profited from the gap between the deposition of one Roman Procurator (Festus) and the arrival of his successor (Albinus), to hand him over for stoning.

As well as the apocryphal Proto-Gospel of James, which exalts the holiness and virginity of Mary, Mother of Jesus, the Letter that bears his name is particularly associated with the name of this James. In the canon of the New Testament, it occupies the first place among the so-called "Catholic Letters," that is, those that were not addressed to any single particular Church—such as Rome, Ephesus, etc.—but to many Churches. It is quite an important writing which heavily insists on the need not to reduce our faith to a purely verbal or abstract declaration, but to express it in practice in good works. Among other things, he invites us to be constant in trials, joyfully accepted, and to pray with trust to obtain from God the gift of wisdom, thanks to which we succeed in understanding that the true values of life are not to be found in transient riches but rather in the ability to share our possessions with the poor and the needy (cf. Jas 1:27).

Thus, St. James's Letter shows us a very concrete and practical Christianity. Faith must be fulfilled in life, above all, in love of neighbor and especially in dedication to the poor. It is against this background that the famous sentence must be read: "As the body apart from the spirit is dead, so faith apart from works is dead" (Jas 2:26).

General Audience
June 28, 2006

St. Pio de Pietrelcina

(1887–1968; SEPTEMBER 23)

Prayer and charity

Prayer pervades the entire work of Padre Pio. It is, so to speak, the transversal element: it animates every initiative. It is the spiritual strength that moves all and orients all according to charity, which is ultimately God himself. God is love. Therefore, the fundamental binomial that I want to repropose to your attention is what is at the center of my Encyclical: love of God and love of neighbor, prayer and charity (cf. *Deus Caritas Est*, nos. 16-18). . . . The Gospel does not allow shortcuts. Whoever addresses the God of Jesus Christ is spurred to serve the brethren; and vice versa, whoever dedicates himself or herself to the poor, discovers there the mysterious Face of God. . . .

Padre Pio has been above all a "man of God." From childhood he felt called by him and responded "with all his heart, with all his soul and with all his strength" (cf. Dt 6:5). Thus, divine love was able to take possession of his humble person and make of him an elect instrument of his salvific design. Praise be to God, who in every age chooses simple and generous souls to accomplish great things (cf. Lk 1:48-49)! In the Church all comes from God, and without him nothing can stand. The works of Padre Pio offer an extraordinary example of this truth. . . . [He is] the man of God, who looked at reality with the eyes of faith and with great hope, because he knew that nothing is impossible to God.

Address on the fiftieth anniversary of the
charitable works of St. Pio de Pietrelcina
October 14, 2006

St. Polycarp of Smyrna

(69–155; FEBRUARY 23)

Eucharist and witness

I would like to reflect on a notion dear to the early Christians, which also speaks eloquently to us today: namely, witness even to the offering of one's own life, to the point of martyrdom. Throughout the history of the Church, this has always been seen as the culmination of the new spiritual worship: "Offer your bodies" (Rom 12:1). One thinks, for example, of the account of the martyrdom of St. Polycarp of Smyrna, a disciple of St. John: the entire drama is described as a liturgy, with the martyr himself becoming Eucharist.

Apostolic Exhortation The Sacrament of Charity
(Sacramentum Caritatis), *no. 85*
February 22, 2007

St. Rafael Guízar y Valencia

(1878–1938; JUNE 6)

Bishop of the poor

St. *Rafael Guízar y Valencia*, Bishop of Vera Cruz in the beloved Mexican Nation, [is] an example of one who has left all to "follow Jesus." This Saint was faithful to the divine Word, "living and active," that penetrates the depth of the spirit (cf. Heb 4:12). Imitating the poor Christ, he renounced his goods and never accepted the gifts of the powerful, or rather, he gave them back immediately. This is why he received "a hundredfold" and could thus help the poor, even amid endless "persecutions" (cf. Mk 10:30). His charity, lived to a heroic degree, earned him the name "Bishop of the poor." In his priestly and later episcopal ministry, he was an untiring preacher of popular missions, the most appropriate way at the time to evangelize people, using his own "Catechism of Christian Doctrine." Since the formation of priests was one of his priorities, he reopened the seminary, which he considered "the apple of his eye," and therefore he would often say: "A Bishop can do without the miter, the crosier and even without the cathedral, but he cannot do without the seminary, since the future of his Diocese depends on it." With this profound sense of priestly paternity he faced new persecutions and exiles, but he always guaranteed the formation of the students. The example of St. Rafael Guízar y Valencia is a call to his brother Bishops and priests to consider as fundamental in pastoral programs, beyond the spirit of poverty and evangelization, the promotion of priestly and religious vocations, and their formation according to the heart of Jesus!

Homily at Mass for the canonization of
St. Rafael Guízar y Valencia and others
October 15, 2006

St. Rose Venerini

(1656–1728; MAY 7)

At the service of education

St. *Rose Venerini* is another example of a faithful disciple of Christ, ready to give up all in order to do the will of God. She loved to say: "I find myself so bound to the divine will that neither death nor life is important: I want to live as he wishes and I want to serve him as he likes, and nothing more" (*Biografia Andreucci*, 515). From here, from this surrender to God, sprang the long-admired work that she courageously developed in favor of the spiritual elevation and authentic emancipation of the young women of her time. St. Rose did not content herself with providing the girls an adequate education, but she was concerned with ensuring their complete formation, with sound references to the Church's doctrinal teaching. Her own apostolic style continues to characterize the life of the Congregation of the Religious Teachers Venerini which she founded. And how timely and important for today's society is this service, which puts them in the field of education and especially of the formation of women.

> *Homily at Mass for the canonization*
> *of St. Rose Venerini and others*
> *October 15, 2006*

SS. Simon and Jude

With an open heart

Simon the Cananaean and Jude Thaddaeus (not to be confused with Judas Iscariot): Let us look at them together, not only because they are always placed next to each other in the lists of the Twelve [cf. Mt 10:3, 4; Mk 3:18; Lk 6:15; Acts 1:13], but also because there is very little information about them. . . . Simon is given a nickname that varies in the four lists: while Matthew and Mark describe him as a "Cananaean," Luke instead describes him as a "Zealot." In fact, the two descriptions are equivalent because they mean the same thing: indeed, in Hebrew the verb "*qanà*" means "to be jealous, ardent" and can be said both of God, since he is jealous with regard to his Chosen People (cf. Ex 20:5), and of men who burn with zeal in serving the one God with unreserved devotion, such as Elijah (cf. 1 Kgs 19:10). . . .

Then with regard to Jude Thaddaeus. . . . very little about him has come down to us. John alone mentions a question he addressed to Jesus at the Last Supper: Thaddaeus says to the Lord: "Lord, how is it that you will manifest yourself to us and not to the world?" This is a very timely question which we also address to the Lord: why did not the Risen One reveal himself to his enemies in his full glory in order to show that it is God who is victorious? Why did he only manifest himself to his disciples? Jesus' answer is mysterious and profound. The Lord says: "If a man loves me, he will keep my word, and my Father will love him, and we will come to him and make our home with him" (Jn 14:22-23). This means that the Risen One must be seen, must be perceived also by the heart, in a way so that God may take up his abode within us. The Lord does not appear as a thing. He desires to enter our lives, and therefore his manifestation is a manifestation that implies and presupposes an open heart. Only in this way do we see the Risen One.

General Audience
October 11, 2006

St. Simon of Lipnica

(1340/1345–1482; JULY 18)

In favor of the poor

Simon of Lipnica, a great son of Poland, a witness of Christ and a follower of the spirituality of St. Francis of Assisi, lived in a distant age but precisely today is held up to the Church as a timely model of a Christian who—enlivened by the spirit of the Gospel—was ready to dedicate his life to his brethren. Thus, filled with the mercy he drew from the Eucharist, he did not hesitate to help the sick who were struck by the plague, and he himself contracted this disease which led to his death. Today in particular, let us entrust to his protection those who are suffering from poverty, illness, loneliness and social injustice. Let us ask through his intercession for the grace of persevering and active love, for Christ and for our brothers and sisters.

Homily at Mass for the canonization of
St. Simon of Lipnica and others
June 3, 2007

St. Stephen

(FIRST CENTURY; DECEMBER 26)

The proto-martyr

St. Stephen [is] the first martyr. . . . Just as Jesus on the Cross entrusted himself to the Father without reserve and pardoned those who killed him, at the moment of his death St. Stephen prayed: "Lord Jesus, receive my spirit"; and further: "Lord, do not hold this sin against them" (cf. Acts 7:59-60). Stephen was a genuine disciple of Jesus and imitated him perfectly. With Stephen began that long series of martyrs who sealed their faith by offering their lives, proclaiming with their heroic witness that God became man to open the Kingdom of Heaven to humankind.

In the atmosphere of Christmas joy, the reference to the Martyr St. Stephen does not seem out of place. Indeed, the shadow of the Cross was already extending over the manger in Bethlehem. It was foretold by the poverty of the stable in which the infant wailed, the prophecy of Simeon concerning the sign that would be opposed and the sword destined to pierce the heart of the Virgin, and Herod's persecution that would make necessary the flight to Egypt. It should not come as a surprise that this Child, having grown to adulthood, would one day ask his disciples to follow him with total trust and faithfulness on the Way of the Cross. Already at the dawn of the Church, many Christians, attracted by his example and sustained by his love, were to witness to their faith by pouring out their blood. The first martyrs would be followed by others down the centuries to our day. How can we not recognize that professing the Christian faith demands the heroism of the Martyrs in our time too, in various parts of the world? Moreover, how can we not say that everywhere, even where there is no persecution, there is a high price to pay for consistently living the Gospel?

Angelus
December 26, 2005

St. Teresa of Avila

(1515–1582; OCTOBER 15)

God alone is changeless

"Everything passes, God never changes," the great spiritual master Teresa of Avila wrote in one of her famous texts. And in the face of the widespread need to get away from the daily routine of sprawling urban areas in search of places conducive to silence and meditation, monasteries of contemplative life offer themselves as "oases" in which human beings, pilgrims on earth, can draw more easily from the wellsprings of the Spirit and quench their thirst along the way. Thus, these apparently useless places are on the contrary indispensable, like the green "lungs" of a city: they do everyone good, even those who do not visit them and may not even know of their existence.

Angelus
November 19, 2006

St. Teresa Benedicta of the Cross (Edith Stein)

(1891–1942; JANUARY 8)

Witness to goodness

[The memorial inscription in German at Auschwitz] evokes the face of Edith Stein, Theresia Benedicta a Cruce: a woman, Jewish and German, who disappeared along with her sister into the black night of the Nazi-German concentration camp; as a Christian and a Jew, she accepted death with her people and for them. The Germans who had been brought to Auschwitz-Birkenau and met their death here were considered as *Abschaum der Nation*—the refuse of the nation. Today we gratefully hail them as witnesses to the truth and goodness which even among our people were not eclipsed. We are grateful to them, because they did not submit to the power of evil, and now they stand before us like lights shining in a dark night. With profound respect and gratitude, then, let us bow our heads before all those who, like the three young men in Babylon facing death in the fiery furnace, could respond: "Only our God can deliver us. But even if he does not, be it known to you, O King, that we will not serve your gods and we will not worship the golden statue that you have set up" (cf. Dan 3:17ff.).

Address at Auschwitz-Birkenau
May 28, 2006

St. Théodore Guérin

(1798–1856; MAY 14)

On mission

"Go, sell everything you own, and give the money to the poor . . . then come, follow me." These words have inspired countless Christians throughout the history of the Church to follow Christ in a life of radical poverty, trusting in Divine Providence. Among these generous disciples of Christ was a young Frenchwoman, who responded unreservedly to the call of the divine Teacher. Mother *Théodore Guérin* entered the Congregation of the Sisters of Providence in 1823, and she devoted herself to the work of teaching in schools. Then, in 1839, she was asked by her Superiors to travel to the United States to become the head of a new community in Indiana. After their long journey over land and sea, the group of six Sisters arrived at St. Mary-of-the-Woods. There they found a simple log-cabin chapel in the heart of the forest. They knelt down before the Blessed Sacrament and gave thanks, asking God's guidance upon the new foundation. With great trust in Divine Providence, Mother Théodore overcame many challenges and persevered in the work that the Lord had called her to do. By the time of her death in 1856, the Sisters were running schools and orphanages throughout the State of Indiana. In her own words, "How much good has been accomplished by the Sisters of St. Mary-of-the-Woods! How much more good they will be able to do if they remain faithful to their holy vocation!" Mother

Théodore Guérin is a beautiful spiritual figure and a model of the Christian life. She was always open for the missions the Church entrusted to her, and she found the strength and the boldness to put them [the missions] into practice in the Eucharist, in prayer and in an infinite trust in Divine Providence. Her inner strength moved her to address particular attention to the poor, and above all to children.

Homily at Mass for the canonization
of St. Théodore Guérin and others
October 15, 2006

St. Thérèse of Lisieux

(1873–1897; OCTOBER 1)

The simple way

St. Teresa of the Child Jesus, the Carmelite virgin and doctor of the Church . . . is universal Co-Patroness of the Missions, together with St. Francis Xavier. May she, who pointed out trusting abandonment to God's love as the "simple" way to holiness, help us to be credible witnesses of the Gospel of charity.

Angelus
October 1, 2006

St. Thomas the Apostle

(FIRST CENTURY; JULY 3)

Seeing through believing

The proverbial scene of the doubting Thomas that occurred eight days after Easter is very well known. At first he did not believe that Jesus had appeared in his absence and said: "Unless I see in his hands the print of the nails, and place my finger in the mark of the nails, and place my hand in his side, I will not believe" (Jn 20:25). Basically, from these words emerges the conviction that Jesus can now be recognized by his wounds rather than by his face. Thomas holds that the signs that confirm Jesus' identity are now above all his wounds, in which he reveals to us how much he loved us. In this the Apostle is not mistaken. As we know, Jesus reappeared among his disciples eight days later and this time Thomas was present. Jesus summons him: "Put your finger here, and see my hands; and put out your hand, and place it in my side; do not be faithless, but believing" (Jn 20:27). Thomas reacts with the most splendid profession of faith in the whole of the New Testament: "My Lord and my God!" (Jn 20:28). . . .

The Apostle Thomas's case is important to us for at least three reasons: first, because it comforts us in our insecurity; second, because it shows us that every doubt can lead to an outcome brighter than any uncertainty; and, lastly, because the words that Jesus addressed to him remind us of the true meaning of mature faith and encourage us to persevere, despite the difficulty, along our journey of adhesion to him.

General Audience
September 27, 2006

St. Thomas Aquinas

(C. 1225–1274; JANUARY 28)

Faith and reason

Today the liturgical calendar commemorates St. Thomas Aquinas, the great Doctor of the Church. With his charism as a philosopher and theologian, he offered an effective model of harmony between reason and faith, dimensions of the human spirit that are completely fulfilled in the encounter and dialogue with one another. According to St. Thomas's thought, human reason, as it were, "breathes": it moves within a vast open horizon in which it can express the best of itself. When, instead, man reduces himself to thinking only of material objects or those that can be proven, he closes himself to the great questions about life, himself and God and is impoverished. The relationship between faith and reason is a serious challenge to the currently dominant culture in the Western world, and for this very reason our beloved John Paul II decided to dedicate an Encyclical to it, entitled, precisely, *Fides et Ratio*—Faith and Reason. Recently, I too returned to this topic in my Discourse to the University of Regensburg.

In fact, the modern development of the sciences brings innumerable positive effects, as we all see, that should always be recognized. At the same time, however, it is necessary to admit that the tendency to consider true only what can be experienced constitutes a limitation of human reason and produces a terrible schizophrenia now acclaimed, which has led to the coexistence of rationalism and materialism, hyper-technology and unbridled instinct. It is urgent, therefore, to rediscover anew human rationality open to the light of the divine *Logos* and his perfect revelation which is Jesus Christ, Son of God made man. When Christian faith is authentic, it does not diminish freedom and human reason; so, why should faith and reason fear one another if the best way for them to express themselves is by meeting and entering into dialogue? Faith presupposes reason and perfects it, and reason, enlightened by faith, finds the strength to rise to knowledge of God and spiritual realities. Human reason loses nothing by opening itself to the content of faith, which, indeed, requires its free and conscious adherence.

St. Thomas Aquinas, with farsighted wisdom, succeeded in establishing a fruitful confrontation with the Arab and Hebrew thought of his time, to the point that he was considered an ever up-to-date teacher of dialogue with other cultures and religions. He knew how to present that wonderful Christian synthesis of reason and faith which today too, for the Western civilization, is a precious patrimony to draw from for an effective dialogue with the great cultural and religious traditions of the East and South of the world. Let us pray that Christians, especially those who work in an academic and cultural context, are able to express the reasonableness of their faith and witness to it in a dialogue inspired by love.

Angelus
January 28, 2007

St. Toribio of Mongrovejo

(1538–1606; MARCH 23)

A missionary spirit

St. Toribio distinguished himself by his selfless dedication to building up and strengthening of the ecclesial communities of his time. He did this with a great spirit of communion and collaboration, always seeking unity, as seen in his convoking of the Third Provincial Council of Lima (1582-1583), which left a precious patrimony of doctrine and pastoral norms. One of its most precious fruits was the so-called *Catechism of St. Toribio*, which has shown itself to be an extraordinarily effective instrument of instruction for millions of persons throughout the centuries, presenting that instruction in a solid way and in conformity with the authentic doctrine of the Church, thus uniting all in a most profound manner, beyond any differences, because they all have "one Lord, one faith, one Baptism" (Eph 4:5). . . . The profound missionary spirit of St. Toribio is manifested in some significant details, like his effort to learn different languages, with a view to preaching personally to all who were entrusted to his pastoral care. He was also a model of respect for the dignity of every human person, whatever his condition, in this way always seeking to arouse the happiness that comes from experiencing oneself as a true son of God.

> *Message for the fourth centenary of the*
> *death of St. Toribio of Mongrovejo*
> *March 23, 2006*

CALENDAR

The saints in this book are listed here by their feast days.

January

2	SS. Basil and Gregory Nazianzen
5	St. Charles of St. Andrew Houben
10	St. Gregory of Nyssa
13	St. Hilary of Poitiers
24	St. Francis de Sales
28	St. Thomas Aquinas
31	St. John Bosco

February

8	St. Josephine Bakhita
14	SS. Cyril and Methodius
21	St. Peter Damian
23	St. Polycarp of Smyrna

March

10	St. Marie Eugenie of Jesus Milleret
18	St. Cyril of Jerusalem
19	St. Joseph
23	St. Toribio of Mongrovejo

April

2	St. Francis of Paola
4	St. Gaetano Catanoso
16	St. Bernadette Soubirous
21	St. Anselm of Canterbury

May

2	St. Athanasius
3	SS. Philip and James
7	St. Rose Venerini
14	St. Matthias; St. Théodore Guérin
25	St. Mary Magdalene de' Pazzi
31	St. Felix of Nicosia

June

1	St. Justin
4	St. Filippo Smaldone
6	St. Rafael Guizar y Valencia
9	St. Ephrem
11	St. Barnabas
22	St. Paulinus of Nola
24	St. John the Baptist
25	St. Maximus of Turin
26	St. Josemaria Escriva de Balaguer
27	St. Cyril of Alexandria
28	St. Irenaeus of Lyons
29	SS. Peter and Paul

July

3	St. Thomas the Apostle
11	St. Benedict of Nursia (Abbot)
18	St. Simon of Lipnica
22	St. Mary Magdalene
23	St. Bridget
25	St. James

| 26 | St. George Preca |
| 31 | St. Ignatius of Loyola |

August

2	St. Eusebius of Vercelli
9	St. Teresa Benedicta of the Cross (Edith Stein)
11	St. Clare
18	St. Albert Hurtado Cruchaga, SJ
20	St. Bernard of Clairvaux
24	St. Bartholomew
27	St. Monica
28	St. Augustine; St. Daniel Comboni

September

3	St. Gregory the Great
12	St. Mary
13	St. John Chrysostom
21	St. Matthew
23	St. Pio de Pietrelcina
29	Archangels Michael, Gabriel, and Raphael
30	St. Jerome

October

1	St. Thérèse of Lisieux
4	St. Francis of Assisi
6	St. Bruno
15	St. Teresa of Avila
17	St. Ignatius of Antioch
28	SS. Simon and Jude

November

December

INDEX

Mothers, Christian: 108
Prayer: 26-27, 92-93, 119
Scripture, Sacred: 4-5, 77-78
Seminary: 122
Service: 86
Silence: 29, 87-88
Solitude: 26, 113
Spiritual life: 65-66
Theology: 21, 29
Truth:
    search for, 8, 14-15, 92-93
Witness: 4, 81, 83, 103, 116,
Word:
    centrality of, 33-34
    of God, 77-78

RELATED TITLES

Pope Benedict XVI: Spiritual Thoughts

Spiritual Thoughts captures Pope Benedict XVI's spiritual life and his extraordinary intelligence as expressed in the first year of his papacy. His thoughts begin to unlock the mystery of his papal legacy. The short reflections from his talks, homilies, and writings are prayerful, sometimes forceful, and always satisfying.
English: No. 5-765, 128 pp.

St. Paul
Spiritual Thoughts Series
Unite yourselves with Christ! Let Pope Benedict XVI teach you how to share the gift of Christ with the world like St. Paul did. Every page has a thought from the Pope about St. Paul's life and writings. Use the space in the book to record your own thoughts. Read, grow your biblical literacy, and dive into St. Paul's writings. A book for everyone seeking Christ.
English: No. 7-053, 128 pp.

Mary
Spiritual Thoughts Series
Embrace Mary, the Mother of God and all Christians! Pope Benedict XVI shares his thoughts on Mary as the Mother of God in this book. Let the Holy Father's explanation of the special Catholic understanding of Mary's mystery enrich your faith journey. For all Christians who want to learn more about Mary.
English: No. 7-054, 168 pp.

To order these resources or to obtain a catalog of other USCCB titles, visit *www.usccbpublishing.org* or call toll-free 800-235-8722. In the Washington metropolitan area or from outside the United States, call 202-722-8716. Para pedidos en español, llame al 800-235-8722 y presione 4 para hablar con un representante del servicio al cliente en español.